Lingua Latina A2
Latin – English
Interlinear Ghost Stories

Latin A2 Reader

Brian Smith

Copyright 2024

Brian Smith

Spectrum et Nuptiae Magicae   4

Mysterium Domus Veteris   20

Manes Colossi   32

Silvae Umbraeque Aeternae   43

Ludi Spectri Aurei   60

Iter Aeliae   76

Saga Veteris Magicae   86

Villa Spectris Lusor   96

Nox ad Murum Hadriani   111

Spectra et Servus   122

Umbrae Templi Baalis   138

Clavis Aeterni   149

Silvae Mysteria   160

Spectra Alexandrina   174

Umbra Hannibalis   185

Spectrum et Nuptiae Magicae

Spectrum Nuptiarum

In urbe Roma, multis annis ante, Titus, mercatoris dives filius, et Laelia, nobilis sed pauperis familiae filia, vivebant. Pater Titi, mercator, mare timet. "Piratae," inquit, "fortunas nostras auferre possunt!"

In the city of Rome, many years ago, Titus, the rich son of a merchant, and Laelia, the daughter of a noble but poor family, lived. Titus's father, the merchant, fears the sea. "Pirates," he says, "could take away our fortunes!"

Laelia, pulchra et sapientia plena, spem suae familiae sustinet. Domus eorum, quae olim divitiis plena erat, nunc in paupertatem delapsa est. "Laelia," pater eius dicit, "diviti nubere debes!"

Laelia, full of beauty and wisdom, sustains the hope of her family. Their house, once full of riches, has now fallen into poverty. "Laelia," her father says, "you must marry a rich man!"

Prope Romam, in villa antiqua, spectrum habitat. Hoc spectrum non est ut cetera; ludere amat, homines terrere et adiuvare potest. Una nocte, ad Titum in somnis venit. "Tite," spectrum dicit, "auxilio tibi ero!"

Near Rome, in an old villa, a ghost resides. This ghost is not like others; it loves to play, can scare people, and also help them. One night, it appears to Titus in a dream. "Titus," the ghost says, "I will help you!"

Eadem nocte, Laelia de Tito somniat. Mirabile! Numquam eum vidit. Sed cor eius tangitur. "Quis est hic Titus?" se ipsa interrogat.

That same night, Laelia dreams of Titus. Amazing! She has never seen him. But her heart is touched. "Who is this Titus?" she asks herself.

Interea, pater Laeliae consilium capit. "Filium divitis invenire debemus," inquit. "Laelia nostra diviti nubere debet."

Meanwhile, Laelia's father makes a plan. "We must find the son of a rich man," he says. "Our Laelia must marry a rich man."

Titus autem, de vero amore meditans, se interrogat: "Ubi est amor meus verus?" Eodem tempore, idem spectrum consilium capit. "Titum et Laeliam coniungere in animo habeo," secum cogitat.

But Titus, thinking about true love, asks himself: "Where is my true love?" At the same time, the same ghost makes a plan. "I intend to unite Titus and Laelia," it thinks to itself.

Mercator, Titi pater, nuntium dirum accipit. "Piratae appropinquant!" exclamat. "Omnia amittere possumus!"

The merchant, Titus's father, receives terrible news. "Pirates are approaching!" he exclaims. "We could lose everything!"

Sed in domo Laeliae, nova spes nascitur. Convivium grande instituunt, sperantes divites Romae convocare. "Forsan," Laelia dicit, "hic inveniam virum qui nos salvare possit."

But in Laelia's house, new hope is born. They organize a great feast, hoping to gather the rich of Rome. "Perhaps," Laelia says, "here I will find the man who can save us."

Ita fabula nostra incipit, spe, amore, et ludis spectralibus plena, ubi antiqua Roma magiae et mysteriis impletur.

Thus, our story begins, full of hope, love, and spectral games, where ancient Rome is filled with magic and mysteries.

Lusus Spectri Incipit

Nocte, cum luna plena luce splendente, spectrum iterum ad Titum venit. "Sequere me," susurrat. Titus, somno adhuc in oculis gravatus, surrexit et ambulare coepit, nesciens quo iret.

At night, with the full moon shining brightly, the ghost came again to Titus. "Follow me," it whispered. Titus, still heavy with sleep in his eyes, got up and began to walk, not knowing where he was going.

In hortos magnos et formosos intravit. Ibi Laelia, quae dormire non poterat, deambulabat. Subito Titum conspicit. "Quis es?" inquit, mirans.

He entered large and beautiful gardens. There, Laelia, who could not sleep, was walking. Suddenly, she spotted Titus. "Who are you?" she asked, astonished.

Titus, expergefactus, circumspicit et Laeliam videt; cor eius exsultat. "Formosa es," inquit, "sed puto me perdidisse."

Titus, now fully awake, looked around and saw Laelia; his heart leaped. "You are beautiful," he said, "but I think I am lost."

Spectrum celatum ridet ventosque et sonos fingit. Titus et Laelia, metu perterriti, se abscondunt. "Quid est hoc?" exclamat Laelia.

The hidden ghost laughed and made wind and sounds. Titus and Laelia, terrified, hid themselves. "What is this?" Laelia exclaimed.

Sub magnam arborem currunt et ibi se occultant. Tum spectrum lumen magicum efficit. Sub hoc lumine, alter alterius vultum clarius videt.

They ran under a large tree and hid there. Then the ghost created a magical light. Under this light, they saw each other's faces more clearly.

"Quid te huc adduxit?" Laelia Titum interrogat. Ille respondet, "Nescio. Somnio te vidi."

"What brought you here?" Laelia asked Titus. He replied, "I don't know. I saw you in a dream."

Laelia de sua familia et difficultatibus narrat. "Pater meus me diviti maritare vult."

Laelia told him about her family and their difficulties. "My father wants me to marry a rich man."

Titus de se et de suo patre mercatore narrat. "Ego quoque somniis ducor," inquit.

Titus told her about himself and his father, the merchant. "I too am led by dreams," he said.

Spectrum, auditis eorum verbis, consilium suum perficere statuit. Subito, animalia nocturna eos circumdant, terrorem incutientia. "Quid agemus?" Laelia interrogat.

The ghost, hearing their words, decided to carry out its plan. Suddenly, nocturnal animals surrounded them, striking fear. "What shall we do?" Laelia asked.

Mox, ad antiquam villam perducti sunt. "Ubi nos nunc sumus?" Titus interrogat. Ibi spectra conspiciunt et magis timore affecti sunt.

Soon, they were led to an old villa. "Where are we now?" Titus asked. There they saw more ghosts and became even more frightened.

"Sed nolite timere," spectrum dicit. "Auxilio vobis ero."

"But do not fear," the ghost said. "I will help you."

In antiqua villa, sub magica luce et nocturnis animalibus, nova pars fabulae incipit. Spectrum, Titus, et Laelia mysteriis et magia involvuntur, novum caput in historia nostra aperientes.

In the old villa, under magical light and surrounded by nocturnal animals, a new part of the story begins. The ghost, Titus, and Laelia are enveloped in mysteries and magic, opening a new chapter in our tale.

Auxilium Spectri et Pericula

Mane, apud villam spectri, Titus et Laelia expergiscuntur. Sol lucet, avesque cantant. "Ubi sumus?" Laelia rogat.

In the morning, at the ghost's villa, Titus and Laelia wake up. The sun shines, and the birds sing. "Where are we?" Laelia asks.

Spectrum advenit. "Salvete!" inquit. "Hodie historiam huius loci narrabo."

The ghost arrives. "Greetings!" it says. "Today, I will tell you the history of this place."

Mercator, Titus pater, villam ingreditur. "Tite!" exclamat. "Ubi te celas?"

The merchant, Titus's father, enters the villa. "Titus!" he exclaims. "Where are you hiding?"

Simul, pater Laeliae nuntium de convivio accepit. "Convivium prosperum fuit," laetus annuntiat.

At the same time, Laelia's father receives news about the feast. "The feast was successful," he announces happily.

Mercator et pater Laeliae conveniunt, de matrimonio et divitiis colloquuntur. "Oportet," mercator suggerit, "ut liberi nostri bene nubant."

The merchant and Laelia's father meet and discuss marriage and wealth. "It is fitting," the merchant suggests, "that our children marry well."

Spectro audiente, consilium proponunt: "Thesaurum antiquum quaerere debemus."

With the ghost listening, they propose a plan: "We must seek an ancient treasure."

Titus, Laelia, et spectrum in locum occultum pergunt. "Hic pericula latent," spectrum admonet.

Titus, Laelia, and the ghost head to a hidden place. "Dangers lie here," the ghost warns.

Itinere peracto, enigmata ardua solvunt, spectrumque eis in periculis superandis adiuvat.

After completing their journey, they solve difficult riddles, and the ghost helps them overcome dangers.

Dum via peragratur, Titus et Laelia de amore suo confabulantur. "Forsitan," Titus susurrat, "nos vere amamus."

As they travel, Titus and Laelia talk about their love. "Perhaps," Titus whispers, "we truly love each other."

Mercator et pater Laeliae, de liberis suis anxii, se interrogant: "Quae nunc agunt liberi nostri?"

The merchant and Laelia's father, worried about their children, ask themselves, "What are our children doing now?"

Cum ad thesauri locum perveniunt, custodem inveniunt. Spectrum dicit, "Hoc aenigma solvere oportet."

When they reach the location of the treasure, they find a guardian. The ghost says, "You must solve this riddle."

Titus et Laelia aenigma solvunt, et subito thesaurus se revelat. Exsultatione magna omnes perfunduntur.

Titus and Laelia solve the riddle, and suddenly the treasure is revealed. Everyone is filled with great joy.

Spectrum, secretum revelans, Laeliae dicit: "Ego sum antecessor tuus."

The ghost, revealing a secret, tells Laelia: "I am your ancestor."

Cum thesauro reperto, omnes gaudent, et thesaurus familiae Laeliae restituitur. "Gratias agimus tibi," universi spectro dicunt. Magna celebratio in honorem spectri et recuperatae fortunae fit.

With the treasure found, everyone rejoices, and the treasure is restored to Laelia's family. "We thank you," they all say to the ghost. A great celebration is held in honor of the ghost and the restored fortune.

Hac in fabulae parte, auxilio spectri et amore mutuo, Titus et Laelia non solum familias suas adiuvant sed etiam de futuris felicioribus somniant.

In this part of the story, with the help of the ghost and their mutual love, Titus and Laelia not only help their families but also dream of a happier future.

Amor in Umbra Spectrorum Floret

Cum thesaurum inveniunt, Titus et Laelia valde gaudent. "Quam beati sumus!" Laelia exclamat. Titus eam complexus, "Una omnia superavimus," inquit.

When they find the treasure, Titus and Laelia are very happy. "How fortunate we are!" Laelia exclaims. Titus, embracing her, says, "Together, we have overcome everything."

Spectrum, eos spectans, ridet. "Amoris vestri benedictio sit," inquit. "Feliciter semper vivatis."

The ghost, watching them, smiles. "May your love be blessed," it says. "May you live happily ever after."

Mercator et pater Laeliae, invento thesauro, de matrimonio sermocinantur. "Consentimus," affirmant. "Titus et Laelia in matrimonium iungantur!"

The merchant and Laelia's father, with the treasure found, talk about marriage. "We agree," they affirm. "Titus and Laelia shall be married!"

Sed piratae, thesauro rumore audito, ad villam contendunt. "Thesaurum nostrum sumemus," minitantur.

But the pirates, having heard rumors of the treasure, head to the villa. "We will take the treasure for ourselves," they threaten.

Spectrum et Titus defensionem parant. Insidias passim disponunt. "Piratas non formidamus," Titus proclamat.

The ghost and Titus prepare for defense. They set up traps everywhere. "We do not fear the pirates," Titus proclaims.

Laelia et mater eius, interea, nuptias magnifice ordinant. Flores, cibum, musicam - nihil deest.

Meanwhile, Laelia and her mother are magnificently preparing the wedding. Flowers, food, music – nothing is missing.

Spectrum, silvis occultatum, piratas perterret. Ventos et voces fingit. "Quid istud est?" piratae exclamant, metu capti.

The ghost, hidden in the woods, frightens the pirates. It creates winds and voices. "What is this?" the pirates exclaim, seized by fear.

Titus, gladio armatus, fortiter resistit. "Hic stamus!" exclamat. Piratas fugat.

Titus, armed with a sword, bravely resists. "Here we stand!" he shouts. He drives the pirates away.

Nuptiae magna cum laetitia celebrantur. Universi felices sunt. "Amor omnia vincit," Titus et Laelia pronuntiant.

The wedding is celebrated with great joy. Everyone is happy. "Love conquers all," Titus and Laelia proclaim.

Spectrum, ad nuptias intuens, ludos mirabilesque efficit. Lux musicaque caelestis - omnes stupent.

The ghost, watching the wedding, creates marvelous tricks. Heavenly light and music – everyone is amazed.

Piratae, confusi atque territi, effugiunt. Thesaurum deserunt. "Locum hunc relinquamus!" vociferantur.

The pirates, confused and terrified, flee. They abandon the treasure. "Let us leave this place!" they shout.

Amor inter Titum et Laeliam per haec discrimina augetur. "Nihil nos dividet," dicunt, manibus coniunctis.

The love between Titus and Laelia grows through these trials. "Nothing will divide us," they say, holding hands.

Post nuptias celebratas, familiis unitis, prosperitas et felicitas adveniunt. "Vita nova incipit," omnes annuntiant.

After the wedding is celebrated, with the families united, prosperity and happiness come. "A new life begins," they all announce.

Spectrum, opere suo consummato, caelum intuetur. "Pax nunc in hac villa manet," murmurat.

The ghost, its work completed, looks toward the sky. "Now peace remains in this villa," it murmurs.

Pax et hilaritas in villa dominatur. Risus, cantus, amorque undique florent. Nova vita plena amoris speique pro Tito et Laelia oritur.

Peace and joy reign in the villa. Laughter, songs, and love bloom everywhere. A new life full of love and hope arises for Titus and Laelia.

Fabula Crescit

Post nuptias, Titus negotium patris adiuvare studet. "Pater," inquit Titus, "adiuvare te cupio."

After the wedding, Titus seeks to help his father's business. "Father," Titus says, "I want to assist you."

Laelia, amorem in oculis gerens, ad eum spectat. "Et de nostra progenie futura cogitamus," ait.

Laelia, with love in her eyes, looks at him. "And we are thinking about our future children," she says.

Spectrum tamen, quod vigil semper est, novum periculum cernit. "Cavete," Titum Laeliamque monet spectrum, "falsus amicus inter vos versatur."

However, the ghost, which is always watchful, sees a new danger. "Beware," the ghost warns Titus and Laelia, "a false friend moves among you."

Ille falsus amicus, invidia motus, thesaurum fortunasque Titi appetit. "Quomodo thesaurum illorum auferre potero?" secum cogitat.

That false friend, driven by envy, seeks the treasure and fortune of Titus. "How can I take their treasure?" he thinks to himself.

Spectrum, consilium eius audiens, Titum et Laeliam advocat. "Periculum imminet," inquit. "Falsus amicus vos fallere conatur."

The ghost, hearing his plan, calls Titus and Laelia. "Danger is near," it says. "A false friend is trying to deceive you."

Titus et Laelia, prudentia et virtute praediti, statim agunt. "Veritatem detegemus," Titus affirmat. "Nullus nos decipiet."

Titus and Laelia, endowed with wisdom and virtue, act immediately. "We will uncover the truth," Titus affirms. "No one will deceive us."

Ingenio sapientiaque spectri, dolus et fraus revelantur. "Veritas hic est!" exclamat Laelia, falsum amicum demonstrans.

With the ghost's cleverness and wisdom, deceit and fraud are revealed. "The truth is here!" Laelia exclaims, pointing to the false friend.

Falsus amicus, cum detegitur, metu affectus, "Paenitet me," inquit, sed sero est. Ex urbe festinat fugere.

The false friend, when discovered, filled with fear, says, "I am sorry," but it is too late. He hurries to flee the city.

Mercator, gratias spectri auxilio agens, fiduciam maiorem habet. "Te absente," dicit mercatori, "hoc efficere non potuissemus."

The merchant, thanking the ghost for its help, feels greater confidence. "Without you," the merchant says, "we could not have done this."

Familiae Laeliae et Titus nunc arctius coniuncti sunt. Amor fiduciaque inter eos augentur.

The families of Laelia and Titus are now more closely united. Love and trust between them grow.

Spectrum, ut amicus fidus, nova mysteria locosque magicos eis demonstrat. "Accedite," inquit, "multa vos docere volo."

The ghost, as a faithful friend, shows them new mysteries and magical places. "Come closer," it says, "I want to teach you many things."

Titus et Laelia, spectri praeceptis eruditi, magicae artis peritia gaudent. "Mirum!" exclamat Laelia, magia captata.

Titus and Laelia, taught by the ghost's lessons, rejoice in their mastery of the magical arts. "Amazing!" Laelia exclaims, captivated by the magic.

Eorum vita cotidiana nunc magicae plena est mirisque. Omnia possibilia esse videntur.

Their daily life is now full of magic and wonders. Everything seems possible.

Amici vicinique, admirantes virtutes Titi et Laeliae, eos laudant. "Quam beati fortique sunt!" aiunt.

Friends and neighbors, admiring the virtues of Titus and Laelia, praise them. "How happy and strong they are!" they say.

Ad honorem spectri et gratiam auxilii eius, magna celebratio fit. "Gratias tibi agimus," omnes spectro dicunt, "pro omnibus quae nobis praestitisti."

In honor of the ghost and in gratitude for its help, a great celebration is held. "We thank you," everyone says to the ghost, "for everything you have given us."

In hac parte narrationis, magia amoreque intertexti, Titus et Laelia non modo pericula superant sed etiam in vita quotidiana mirabilia experiuntur. Eorum amor ac societas cum spectro crescunt, et omnes in villa feliciores fiunt.

In this part of the story, woven with magic and love, Titus and Laelia not only overcome dangers but also experience wonders in their daily life. Their love and partnership with the ghost grow, and everyone in the villa becomes happier.

Periculum Redivivum

Nuntius ad villam cursitat. "Piratae!" exclamat. "Piratae mox advenient!"

A messenger runs to the villa. "Pirates!" he exclaims. "The pirates will arrive soon!"

Titus, huius nuntii auditu, socios congregat. "Parati debemus esse," affirmat. "Id quod nostrum est defendemus."

Titus, hearing this news, gathers his allies. "We must be ready," he declares. "We will defend what is ours."

Spectrum, consilium eorum audiens, apparet. "Consilium habeo," inquit. "Adiuvabo vos contra piratas pugnare."

The ghost, hearing their plan, appears. "I have an idea," it says. "I will help you fight the pirates."

Nocte, luna illuminante, piratae tacite villam petunt. Insidiarum tamen ignari sunt.

At night, under the shining moon, the pirates quietly approach the villa. However, they are unaware of the traps.

Spectrum, arte magica utendo, illusiones terroresque nocturnos creat. Silva sonos horrendos emittit.

The ghost, using magic, creates illusions and night terrors. The forest emits horrible sounds.

Piratae, perterriti, in insidias incidunt. "Quae sunt haec?" exclamant, sed iam sero est. A civibus facile comprehenduntur.

The pirates, terrified, fall into the traps. "What is this?" they shout, but it is too late. They are easily captured by the townspeople.

In hac confusione, Laelia et Titus non solum fortitudinem demonstrant sed etiam sagacitatem. Piratas ingenio fugant.

In this confusion, Laelia and Titus show not only strength but also cleverness. They drive away the pirates with ingenuity.

Victoria consecuta, tota urbs festivitatem agit. "Victoria!" clamant omnes. Laetitia undique est.

With victory achieved, the whole city celebrates. "Victory!" everyone shouts. Joy is everywhere.

Spectrum, opere suo finito, gaudium suum ostendit. "Novas res inveniam," dicit, ludendi cupidus.

The ghost, its work completed, shows its joy. "I will find new things," it says, eager to play.

Titus et Laelia, sub caelo stellato, de futuris pacisque spe colloquuntur. "Pacem desideramus," Laelia affatur. "Simul omnia superabimus," Titus adiungit.

Titus and Laelia, under the starry sky, talk about the future and hope for peace. "We desire peace," Laelia says. "Together, we will overcome everything," Titus adds.

Mercator, honorifice, piratas iustitiae tradit. "Iustitia est servanda," pronuntiat.

The merchant, with honor, hands over the pirates to justice. "Justice must be upheld," he declares.

Captis piratis, pax securitasque in regionem redit. Omnes tandem spirant, metu liberati.

With the pirates captured, peace and safety return to the region. Everyone finally breathes, freed from fear.

Spectrum, suam cogitans operationem, de posteritate meditatur. "Quae sequentur?" secum quaerit.

The ghost, thinking about its actions, reflects on the future. "What will follow?" it asks itself.

Titus et Laelia, gratitudine moti, spectrum accedunt. "Tibi gratias agimus," dicunt. "Absque te, hoc effici non potuisset."

Titus and Laelia, moved by gratitude, approach the ghost. "We thank you," they say. "Without you, this could not have been done."

Magnifica celebratio gratia victoriae et pacis fit. Epulae, vinum, risusque - omnia ad festum contribuunt.

A magnificent celebration is held in gratitude for victory and peace. Feasts, wine, and laughter – all contribute to the festivity.

Hac in narrationis parte, per virtutem et ingenium, Titus et Laelia non solum piratas vincunt sed etiam pacem securitatemque suae terrae restituunt. Amicitia eorum cum spectro firmatur, demonstrans amorem, fidem, et concordiam etiam in difficillimis temporibus triumphare.

In this part of the story, through courage and ingenuity, Titus and Laelia not only defeat the pirates but also restore peace and security to their land. Their friendship with the ghost is strengthened, showing that love, loyalty, and harmony can triumph even in the most difficult times.

Magicae Vincula

In villa tranquilla, nocte luna plena illustrata, novum periculum surgit. Ludi magici, periculis pleni, imminent.

In the quiet villa, on a night illuminated by the full moon, a new danger arises. Magical games, full of peril, are approaching.

Spectrum Titum et Laeliam ad se vocat. "Ad ultimum proelium vos ducere me oportet," inquit. "Estisne parati?"

The ghost calls Titus and Laelia to itself. "I must lead you to the final battle," it says. "Are you ready?"

Armis magicis instructi, contra novos hostes contendunt. "Magia nostra utamur," Titus suadet. Laelia consentit, "Simul invicti sumus."

Armed with magic, they fight against new enemies. "Let us use our magic," Titus suggests. Laelia agrees, "Together we are invincible."

Nocte illa, sub plenilunio, certamen anceps fit. Circa eos, magia palpabilis est.

On that night, under the full moon, the battle is fierce. Around them, magic is tangible.

"Virtus spectri amorisque vinculum," spectrum affirmat, "magnam potentiam generat." Fide et amore coniuncti, hostes vincunt.

"The strength of the ghost and the bond of love," the ghost declares, "generate great power." United by faith and love, they defeat the enemies.

Pax villaque restituuntur. Omnes dulcedine pacis fruuntur, grato animo.

Peace and the villa are restored. Everyone enjoys the sweetness of peace with grateful hearts.

Titus et Laelia, spectro adstantes, de amoris virtute discunt. "Amor nobis viam monstravit," Laelia memorat. "Nosque tutavit," Titus adicit.

Titus and Laelia, standing beside the ghost, learn about the power of love. "Love showed us the way," Laelia recalls. "And it protected us," Titus adds.

Celebratione ultima, familiares amicique congregantur. Risus cantusque resonant. "Hoc triumphus noster est," universi exclamant.

In the final celebration, family and friends gather. Laughter and songs echo. "This is our triumph," everyone exclaims.

Spectrum, coram omnibus stans, donum ultimum offert. "Portam ad mundos alios vobis trado," inquit.

The ghost, standing before them all, offers its final gift. "I give you the gate to other worlds," it says.

Titus et Laelia, miris pleni, de futuris cogitant. "Quas terras investigabimus?" Laelia susurrat.

Titus and Laelia, filled with wonder, think about the future. "What lands will we explore?" Laelia whispers.

Spectrum, opere suo consummato, ad caelos respicit. "Valete," inquit, et ad aetheras regiones ascendit.

The ghost, its work completed, looks up to the heavens. "Farewell," it says, and ascends to the ethereal realms.

Cuncti, spectantes, valedictionem et gratias agunt. "Tibi gratias agimus," clamant, "pro omnibus quae nobis dedisti!"

Everyone, watching, gives their farewell and thanks. "We thank you," they shout, "for everything you have given us!"

Titus et Laelia, manibus coniunctis, spondent amorem vitamque plenam novarum rerum persequi. "In aeternum coniuncti," affirmant.

Titus and Laelia, holding hands, vow to pursue a life full of new adventures and love. "Joined forever," they affirm.

Cum proeliis superatis, pax et felicitas in urbe villaque manent. Initium vitae novae, spe felicitateque plenae, fit.

With the battles overcome, peace and happiness remain in the city and the villa. The beginning of a new life, full of hope and happiness, begins.

Ita nostra fabula clauditur, omnibus in spe felicitatis futurae viventibus. Amor, fides, amicitiaque, ad ultimum, praevalent.

Thus our story closes, with everyone living in hope of future happiness. Love, faith, and friendship, in the end, prevail.

Mysterium Domus Veteris

Procella Appropinquat

Mercator Romanus, Gaius nomine, et servus Germanicus, Alaricus appellatus, per vastos agros Romani imperii iter faciunt. Caelum nubilum est, ventusque fortiter spirat. "Vide, Alarice! Procella advenit!" exclamat Gaius. Alaricus, flavis capillis et caeruleis oculis, caelum intuetur et respondet, "Ita vero, domine. Festinandum est!"

A Roman merchant, named Gaius, and a Germanic slave, called Alaric, travel through the vast fields of the Roman Empire. The sky is cloudy, and the wind blows strongly. "Look, Alaric! A storm is coming!" Gaius exclaims. Alaric, with blond hair and blue eyes, looks at the sky and responds, "Indeed, master. We must hurry!"

Per agros vastos ambulant, cum procul domum magnam desolatamque conspiciunt. "Illuc confugiamus!" Gaius suadet. Timore procellae moti, ad domum currunt. Mirum! Porta domus aperta est. "Quis hic manet?" Alaricus susurrat. "Nemo. Deserta videtur," Gaius respondet, et ambo intrant.

They walk through the vast fields when, in the distance, they see a large and desolate house. "Let's take refuge there!" Gaius suggests. Moved by fear of the storm, they run to the house. Amazing! The door is open. "Who stays here?" Alaric whispers. "No one. It seems deserted," Gaius responds, and both enter.

Domus antiqua, telis et pulvere plena, est. Sonitus venti per fenestras ruptas audiri potest. "Ubi dormiemus?" Alaricus quaerit. Gaius circumspiciens, "In atrio pernoctabimus. Saltem a vento aliquantulum protegemur," respondet.

The old house is filled with cobwebs and dust. The sound of the wind can be heard through broken windows. "Where will we sleep?" Alaric asks. Gaius, looking around, says, "We will sleep in the atrium. At least we will be somewhat protected from the wind."

Nocte, dum in atrio cubant, sonos insolitos audiunt. "Audisne id, Gaī?" Alaricus, trepidatione motus, susurrat. "Ita," respondet Gaius, "tanquam gradus in superioribus." Ambo in silentio manent, intenti audiunt. Momento post, Gaius addit, "Non soli sumus in hac domo."

At night, while lying in the atrium, they hear strange sounds. "Do you hear that, Gaius?" Alaric whispers, trembling with fear. "Yes," Gaius responds, "like footsteps upstairs." They both remain silent, listening carefully. A moment later, Gaius adds, "We are not alone in this house."

Arcana Obscura

Prima luce, Gaius et Alaricus consilium capiunt ut domum explorarent. "Quid hoc est?" Alaricus curiose interrogat, parietes vetustis imaginibus ornatos inspiciens.

At first light, Gaius and Alaric decide to explore the house. "What is this?" Alaric curiously asks, inspecting the walls adorned with ancient images.

"Antiqui habitatores," Gaius respondet. "Quare autem domus deserta est?"

"The ancient inhabitants," Gaius responds. "But why is the house deserted?"

Progredientes, pallidam feminae statuam in angulo conspiciunt. "Aspice, Gaī, haec statua... tam viva videtur," Alaricus timide dicit.

As they move forward, they notice a pale statue of a woman in the corner. "Look, Gaius, this statue... it seems so lifelike," Alaric says timidly.

"Progrediamur," Gaius hortatur, sed dum ambulant, portas clausas reperiunt. In culina, vasa fracta in solo iacent. "Quis hic cenavit... et quid evenit?" Gaius secum cogitat.

"Let's keep going," Gaius urges, but as they walk, they find closed doors. In the kitchen, broken dishes lie on the floor. "Who dined here... and what happened?" Gaius wonders to himself.

Subito, porta sine causa movetur. "Quis adest?" Alaricus exclamat, sed responsio nulla venit. Solum sonus altus domūs audiri potest.

Suddenly, a door moves for no reason. "Who is there?" Alaric shouts, but no answer comes. Only the loud sound of the house can be heard.

Accedentes ad speculum, umbram praeter naturam vident. "Estne quis nobiscum?" Alaricus, tremens, interrogat.

Approaching a mirror, they see a shadow that is unnatural. "Is someone with us?" Alaric asks, trembling.

Bibliothecam ingressi, librum antiquum inveniunt. "Domus haec... historiae plena est," Gaius murmure dicit, librum tractans. In camīno, sine igne, lumen apparet.

Entering the library, they find an ancient book. "This house... is full of history," Gaius murmurs, handling the book. In the fireplace, without fire, a light appears.

"Vide aquam in vasculo motam!" Alaricus clamat. Voces susurrantes circa eos volitant. "Hoc audis?" Gaius interrogat. Lumina in domo intermittunt, et temperatura loci descendit. "Frigidum est," Alaricus ait, bracchia circum se stringens.

"Look, the water in the vase is moving!" Alaric shouts. Whispering voices float around them. "Do you hear this?" Gaius asks. The lights in the house flicker, and the temperature drops. "It's cold," Alaric says, wrapping his arms around himself.

Bibliotheca relicta, sentiunt quasi aliquid invisibile eos sequatur. "Spiritus est?" Alaricus susurrat.

Leaving the library, they feel as if something invisible is following them. "Is it a spirit?" Alaric whispers.

"Forsitan... sed quid ab nobis vult?" Gaius cogitat.

"Perhaps... but what does it want from us?" Gaius wonders.

Per domum plenam mysteriis et sonis ambulantes, Gaius et Alaricus magis magisque in arcana eius involvuntur, sentientes se non solos esse in hac antiqua structura.

As they walk through the house, full of mysteries and sounds, Gaius and Alaric become more and more entangled in its secrets, feeling that they are not alone in this ancient structure.

Spiritus Se Revelat

Nocte, cum silentium omnia tegit, figura feminea paulatim in umbris se ostendere incipit. Gaius et Alaricus, terrore affecti, umbram cernunt quae, licet muta sit, gestu eos in altiorem cameram ducit.

At night, when silence covers everything, a female figure gradually begins to reveal itself in the shadows. Gaius and Alaric, terrified, see the shadow, which, though silent, gestures them to follow into an upper room.

*"Sequimur hanc?" tremens Alaricus rogat. "Ita, sequimur,"
Gaius confirmat, etiamsi ipse metuat.*

"Shall we follow her?" a trembling Alaric asks. "Yes, we
follow," Gaius confirms, though he himself is afraid.

*In superiore camera, commentariolum antiquum, pulvere
tectum, inveniunt. "De domina domūs... eiusque morte hic
scribitur," Gaius, legens, enarrat. Commentariolum suggerit
spiritum, ipsam dominam, pacem desiderare.*

In the upper room, they find an ancient, dust-covered journal.
"It is written here about the lady of the house... and her death,"
Gaius, reading, explains. The journal suggests that the spirit, the
lady herself, desires peace.

*Dum legunt, subito et sine manifesta causa, omnia in camera
motu incipiunt. Ad exitum Gaius et Alaricus currunt, sed portam
clausam inveniunt. "Exīre non possumus!" clamat Alaricus.*

While they read, suddenly and without apparent cause,
everything in the room begins to move. Gaius and Alaric run to the
exit, but find the door closed. "We can't get out!" Alaric shouts.

*Fenestrae sine causa visibili confringuntur, vocesque iratae per
domum resonant. Lumina repente extinguuntur et mox iterum
accenduntur. Utrumque frigore manuum glacialis tangitur, quasi
spiritus eos contrectet.*

The windows shatter without visible cause, and angry voices
echo through the house. The lights suddenly go out and soon turn
back on again. Both are touched by the chill of icy hands, as if a
spirit is grasping them.

*In speculo inspectantes, vultus mutantur, suos non agnoscunt.
Sine ulla monitione, obiecta in eos iaciuntur, quasi spiritus eos
propellere conetur.*

Looking into the mirror, their faces change, and they no longer
recognize themselves. Without any warning, objects are thrown at
them, as if the spirit is trying to push them out.

Nocte, per somnia, tristis spiritus fabula narratur. De domina domūs Gaius et Alaricus somniant, quomodo vixerit, quomodo periit, et quid quaerat: pacem.

At night, through dreams, the sad tale of the spirit is told. Gaius and Alaric dream of the lady of the house, how she lived, how she died, and what she seeks: peace.

"Adiuvare nos vult," Gaius, expergefactus, dicit. "Forsitan et nos ipsi iuvari possimus, inveniendo solutionem quaesiti eius," Alaricus spe addit.

"She wants to help us," Gaius, having woken up, says. "Perhaps we can also help ourselves by finding the solution to her quest," Alaric adds hopefully.

Ita, nocte repleta terrore revelationibusque, Gaius et Alaricus magis discunt de historia domūs spiritūsque qui eos circumdant. Decernunt modum quaerere quo spiritum adiuvare possint, pacem domui spirituīque sperantes afferre.

Thus, in a night filled with terror and revelations, Gaius and Alaric learn more about the history of the house and the spirits that surround them. They decide to seek a way to help the spirit, hoping to bring peace to both the house and the spirit.

Pacis Questus

Post noctem plenam revelationibus, Gaius et Alaricus mane surgunt, animo firmato ad spiritum adiuvandum. "Quaerere debemus quid spiritus desideret," Gaius, diarium iterum inspiciens, dicit.

After a night full of revelations, Gaius and Alaric rise in the morning, determined to help the spirit. "We must find out what the spirit desires," Gaius says, looking again at the journal.

Ad hortum procedunt, ubi sepulcrum antiquum et lapideum reperiunt. "Ecce," Alaricus indicat, "sepulcrum dominae est." Inscriptionem legunt, quae vitam desideriaque dominae enarrat.

They proceed to the garden, where they find an ancient stone tomb. "Look," Alaric points out, "this is the lady's tomb." They read the inscription, which recounts the life and desires of the lady.

Nocturno tempore, ad sepulcrum redire constituunt. "Hic flores ponamus; fortasse spiritus pacem percipiet," Alaricus proponit. Factum est, et preces pacis spiritui offerunt.

At night, they decide to return to the tomb. "Let's place flowers here; perhaps the spirit will find peace," Alaric suggests. They do so, offering prayers for the spirit's peace.

"Si nos audis, signum da," Gaius in obscuritate susurrat. Subito, coram sepulcro, rosa alba quasi ex nihilo nata apparet. "Signum hoc est!" Alaricus, gaudens, exclamat. Sensus pacis eos afficit, sed mox terra tremit.

"If you hear us, give a sign," Gaius whispers in the darkness. Suddenly, in front of the tomb, a white rose appears as if from nothing. "This is the sign!" Alaric exclaims joyfully. A sense of peace overwhelms them, but soon the ground begins to tremble.

Lux clara sepulcro emanat, vocesque amicae sed maestae audiuntur. "Audire nos videtur... et, fortasse, adiuvare vult," Gaius interpretatur.

A bright light shines from the tomb, and friendly but sorrowful voices are heard. "It seems to hear us... and perhaps wants to help," Gaius interprets.

Domum reversi, tumultum auctum inveniunt. "Aliquid adhuc est quod solvendum sit," Alaricus asserit, "Non tantum de domina est sermo."

Returning to the house, they find the unrest has increased. "There is still something that must be solved," Alaric asserts. "This is not just about the lady."

Ita spiritu communicantes, Gaius et Alaricus arcanum adhuc domi esse quod solvendum sit intellegunt. Sed nunc sciunt, non solum ipsi sed etiam spiritus pacem solutionemque desiderare. Nova spe fiduciaque instructi, ad reliquum mysterium investigandum solvendumque parati sunt.

Thus, communicating with the spirit, Gaius and Alaric realize that there is still a mystery in the house that must be solved. But now they know that not only they but also the spirit desires peace and resolution. Armed with new hope and confidence, they are ready to investigate and solve the remaining mystery.

Camera Occulta

Gaius et Alaricus, somnio revelatorio permoti, commentariolum iterum scrutantur.

Gaius and Alaric, moved by a revealing dream, examine the journal again.

"Scriptum est de camera secreta," Gaius Alarico narrat. "Forsitan in bibliotheca sit?"

"It is written about a secret room," Gaius tells Alaric. "Perhaps it is in the library?"

In bibliotheca, librum quodam modo tractantes, sonum audire possunt, qui clavi vertentis simillimus est; mox paries movetur, ostiumque secretum aperitur.

In the library, as they handle a certain book, they hear a sound very similar to a turning key; soon the wall moves, and a secret door opens.

"Inventum est!" Alaricus proclamat.

"It has been found!" Alaric proclaims.

Ante eos camera aperitur, rerum antiquarum plena. In eius medio, arca vetusta, pulvere operta, posita est. Accedentes caute, arcam aperiunt et tabulas antiquas de familia domus continentes inveniunt.

Before them, a room opens, full of ancient objects. In its center, there is an old chest, covered with dust. Cautiously approaching, they open the chest and find ancient documents about the house's family.

"Tabulae hae... historiae sunt!" Alaricus exclamat.

"These records... they are histories!" Alaric exclaims.

Documentis inspectis, spiritus feminae apparet, nunc tranquillior quam prius.

After examining the documents, the spirit of the woman appears, now calmer than before.

"Nos intuetur," Gaius susurrat. Documenta demonstrant dominam iniuste accusatam esse:

"She is watching us," Gaius whispers. The documents show that the lady was unjustly accused:

"Innocens fuit," Gaius voce alta dicit.

"She was innocent," Gaius says aloud.

"Spiritus iustitiam petit," Alaricus affirmat. "Veritatem enuntiare debemus."

"The spirit seeks justice," Alaric affirms. "We must reveal the truth."

Inter documenta clavis invenitur, quae ad domus partem alteram ducit. Sequentes clavem, nova indicia verae historiae, quae ad fabulae culmen ducunt, reperiunt.

Among the documents, a key is found, which leads to another part of the house. Following the key, they find new clues about the true story, which lead to the climax of the tale.

"Mysterium hoc solvendum est, pro animae pacificatione, pro domus purificatione," Gaius statuit.

"This mystery must be solved, for the peace of the soul, for the purification of the house," Gaius declares.

Alaricus consentit: "Iustitiam adferemus."

Alaric agrees: "We will bring justice."

Ergo, Gaius et Alaricus, novis indicibus armati et veritatem revelare propositi, ad ultimam narrationis partem procedunt, spe pacem non solum domui sed etiam inhabitanti spiritui afferendi.

Thus, Gaius and Alaric, armed with new clues and determined to reveal the truth, proceed to the final part of the story, hoping to bring peace not only to the house but also to the spirit residing within.

Pacis Redemptio

Nocte ultima in domo, Gaius et Alaricus vigilias agunt. Spiritus dominae apparet, tranquillitas eius manifesta.

On the last night in the house, Gaius and Alaric keep watch. The spirit of the lady appears, her tranquility evident.

"Tranquilla videtur," Alaricus murmure dicit.

"She seems calm," Alaric murmurs.

Subito, spiritus virilis ante eos constitit. "Iste est... reus verus," Gaius submissa voce profert. Statuunt se cum spiritu femineo coniungi ut spiritum virilem confronterent.

Suddenly, a male spirit stands before them. "This is... the true culprit," Gaius says in a low voice. They decide to join forces with the female spirit to confront the male spirit.

"Quid a nobis vis? Cur hic ades?" Gaius interrogat, fortiter.

"What do you want from us? Why are you here?" Gaius asks, boldly.

"Pacem et iustitiam petimus," Alaricus adiungit. Spiritus virilis resistit, oculis ira plenis, sed debilior apparere videtur.

"We seek peace and justice," Alaric adds. The male spirit resists, his eyes full of anger, but he seems to weaken.

Per totam domum lumina micant et soni tonitrui similes audiri possunt. Magna est confusio, sed Gaius et Alaricus constantes stant.

Throughout the house, lights flicker and sounds like thunder can be heard. There is great confusion, but Gaius and Alaric stand firm.

"Discede!" clamant concordes.

"Leave!" they shout together.

Cum verba pacis et iustitiae pronuntiant, spiritus virilis frustratione patet et, luce circumfusus, discedit. Subito, omnis tumultus sistit et domus tranquillitatem profundam recipit.

As they speak words of peace and justice, the male spirit reveals his frustration and, surrounded by light, disappears. Suddenly, all the turmoil stops, and the house returns to a profound calm.

Mane, primo sole fenestras tangente, domus renovata splendet.

In the morning, with the first sunlight touching the windows, the house shines, renewed.

"Renovata videtur," Alaricus admiratur.

"It looks renewed," Alaric marvels.

"Tempus est nos abire," Gaius pronuntiat, sarcinas parans. Egressi, spiritui femineo gratias agunt.

"It's time for us to leave," Gaius declares, packing their belongings. As they leave, they thank the female spirit.

"Pacem repperisti. Tibi gratias agimus," Gaius dicit, Alaricus capite inclinato in signum honoris.

"You have found peace. We thank you," Gaius says, while Alaric bows his head in a gesture of respect.

Exeuntes, novam viam corde pacato capessunt. Domum respicientes, norunt eam nunc pacis locum esse, eius historia expurgata et animis quondam inquietis nunc requiescentibus.

As they leave, they take a new path with peaceful hearts. Looking back at the house, they know it is now a place of peace, its history cleansed and the once restless spirits now at rest.

"Miraculum hoc," Gaius ait, "finis tamen bonus est."

"This is a miracle," Gaius says, "but it's a good ending."

"Verum," Alaricus consentit, "in memoria nostra semper manebit."

"True," Alaric agrees, "it will remain in our memory forever."

Sub orto sole, Gaius et Alaricus novas iterum vias inquirunt, domus veteris historia iam vitae suae parte facta. Domus, quae olim terroris sedes erat, nunc pacis et redemptionis testimonium praebet.

Under the rising sun, Gaius and Alaric seek new paths once more, with the history of the old house now a part of their lives. The house, which was once a place of terror, now stands as a testament to peace and redemption.

Manes Colossi

Mors in Arena

Anno Domini CCCLXXX, in magno Colosseo, tres pugnatores conveniunt: Scythus crinitus rufus, Gothus crinitus flavus, et Suebus. Undique spectatores clamant, intenti pugnam opperiuntur.

In the year 380 AD, in the great Colosseum, three fighters meet: a red-haired Scythian, a blonde-haired Goth, and a Suebi. Spectators shout from all sides, eagerly awaiting the fight.

Scythus, gladio in manu, ad Gothum et Suebum convertitur et dicit: "Hodie, in hac arena, fortitudinem nostram probabimus. Parati estis?"

The Scythian, with a sword in hand, turns to the Goth and the Suebi and says: "Today, in this arena, we will prove our strength. Are you ready?"

Gothus, scuto levato, respondet: "Paratus sum. Mors aut gloria nobis manet."

The Goth, raising his shield, replies: "I am ready. Death or glory awaits us."

Suebus, oculos fixos in arenam, susurrat: "In morte, una stamus. Pugnemus ut leones."

The Suebi, his eyes fixed on the arena, whispers: "In death, we stand as one. Let us fight like lions."

Cum pugna incipit, spectatores fremitum magnum faciunt, et ferrum contra scutum resonans per Colosseum auditur. Pugnatores, viribus paribus, diu pugnant, sudor et sanguis mixti sub sole occidente.

As the fight begins, the spectators roar, and the sound of iron striking against shields echoes through the Colosseum. The fighters, equally matched in strength, battle for a long time, sweat and blood mingling under the setting sun.

Dum umbrae in arena longae fiunt, spectator exclamat: "Videte! Fortitudinem veram!"

As shadows grow long in the arena, a spectator shouts: "Look! True strength!"

Denique omnes tres simul cadunt. Mortui, sed non victi, in arena iacent. Spectatores, commotione pleni, paulatim abeunt, manes pugnatorum ignorantes.

At last, all three fall together. Dead, but not defeated, they lie in the arena. The spectators, filled with emotion, slowly leave, unaware of the warriors' spirits.

Nox venit, et silentium profundum arenae regnat. Sub lumine lunae, tres manes surgunt, oculi eorum inaestuabiles.

Night falls, and deep silence reigns over the arena. Under the moonlight, the three spirits rise, their eyes glowing fiercely.

Manes in medio arenae stant, et Scythus dicit: "Colosseum nostrum est, in aeternum."

The spirits stand in the center of the arena, and the Scythian says: "The Colosseum is ours, forever."

Gothus, ad stellas spectans, affirmat: "Hic manebimus."

The Goth, gazing at the stars, affirms: "Here we shall remain."

Suebus, manum in terram ponens, susurrat: "Semper, semper."

The Suebi, placing his hand on the ground, whispers: "Always, always."

In tenebris, pactum inter eos factum est, ut Colosseum per aeternitatem errarent et quicumque noctu maneret terrerent.

In the darkness, a pact is made between them, to wander the Colosseum for eternity and to haunt anyone who remains there at night.

Noctes Terrae

In umbra cordis Colossi, sub noctis velamine anno MMXXIV, aether gravis erat susurris saeculorum praeteritorum. Marcus et Iulia, duo iuvenes viatores, morati sunt longe postquam portae clausae sunt, capti maiestate loci. Secretum angulum invenientes, ibi, fatigati ex diurna exploratione, somno se dediderunt.

In the shadow of the heart of the Colosseum, under the veil of night in the year 2024, the air was heavy with the whispers of past centuries. Marcus and Julia, two young travelers, lingered long after the gates had closed, captivated by the majesty of the place. Finding a secret corner, they, tired from the day's exploration, gave themselves over to sleep.

Media nocte, cum omnia silerent, tres manes — Scythus crinitus rufus, Gothus crinitus flavus, Suebusque — locum suum antiquum vagabantur, inquieti memoria pugnae quae vitas eorum abstulerat. In tenebris, Marcus et Iulia repente expergefacti sunt, oculis ad tenebras adiustatis.

In the middle of the night, when all was silent, three spirits — the red-haired Scythian, the blonde Goth, and the Suebi — roamed their ancient place, restless with the memory of the battle that had taken their lives. In the darkness, Marcus and Julia suddenly awoke, their eyes adjusting to the shadows.

Marcus, voce tremula, Iuliae susurravit: "Sensistine hoc? Frigiditas nos circumdat, quasi praesentia alicuius antiqui et oblivione digni."

Marcus, in a trembling voice, whispered to Julia: "Did you feel that? A chill surrounds us, as if the presence of something ancient and forgotten."

Iulia, corde pulsante, respondit: "Aliquid nobiscum est. Non soli sumus." Manibus inter se iunctis, in silentio auscultabant, sensu praesentiae alicuius vel alicuius rei invisibilis crescente.

Julia, her heart racing, replied: "Something is with us. We are not alone." Holding each other's hands, they listened in silence, their sense of an unseen presence growing.

Subito, levis aura surrexit, susurros portans vix audibiles. Voces sine corpore, "Cur hic estis?" interrogabant, frigus in aere profundius inducentes.

Suddenly, a light breeze arose, carrying barely audible whispers. Disembodied voices asked, "Why are you here?" deepening the chill in the air.

"Quis est?" Marcus exiguo murmure quaesivit, spem lucis in tenebris quaerens.

"Who is it?" Marcus asked in a faint murmur, hoping for light in the darkness.

Umbrae moventes apparuerunt, formae virorum fortium, sed vacuae et pallidae, eos circumdantes. Tres manes, sua historia narrare cupientes, coeperunt: "Nocte hac, nobiscum manebitis," una voce dixerunt, tono qui simul terrorem et misericordiam movebat.

Moving shadows appeared, the forms of strong men, but hollow and pale, surrounding them. The three spirits, eager to tell their story, began: "Tonight, you will stay with us," they said in one voice, with a tone that stirred both terror and compassion.

Marcus et Iulia, corde ad cor loquentes, steterunt immobiles, historiam spectrorum et loci sui in historia mundi audiendi parati. In nocte Colossi, inter manes et monumenta, dialogus inter praeteritum et praesens, inter vivos et mortuos, incepit.

Marcus and Julia, speaking heart to heart, stood still, ready to hear the story of the spirits and their place in the world's history. In the night of the Colosseum, among the spirits and monuments, a dialogue between past and present, between the living and the dead, began.

Voces Noctis

Manes per umbras errant, fabulas antiquas inter se susurrantes. Luna plena caelum illuminat, lumina pallida per Colosseum diffundentia.

The spirits wander through the shadows, whispering ancient stories to each other. The full moon lights up the sky, spreading pale light through the Colosseum.

Marcus et Iulia, audaces iuvenes, manibus ad manes provocandos accedunt. Subito, sonus catenarum auditur, frigus subitum eos invadit.

Marcus and Julia, brave young ones, approach the spirits with hands extended to challenge them. Suddenly, the sound of chains is heard, and a sudden chill invades them.

"Quid est hic sonitus?" Marcus voce tremula inquit.

"What is this sound?" Marcus asks in a trembling voice.

Iulia, oculos ad umbras dirigens, respondet: "Crede mihi, Marce, animas antiquas provocamus."

Julia, directing her eyes toward the shadows, responds: "Believe me, Marcus, we are provoking ancient souls."

Umbrae longae eos sequuntur, formae terrentes. Marcus, pavore perterritus, exclamat: "Quid vultis a nobis?"

Long shadows follow them, terrifying forms. Marcus, filled with fear, exclaims: "What do you want from us?"

Voces clarae, "Quis nos liberabit?" in aere resonant, Marcus et Iulia perterriti consistunt.

Clear voices resonate in the air, "Who will free us?" Marcus and Julia stop, terrified.

"Non time," Iulia Marcum consolatur, "fortes sumus una. Consilium capiamus, et manes adiuvare conabimur."

"Do not fear," Julia comforts Marcus, "we are strong together. Let's come up with a plan and try to help the spirits."

Ventus repente per muros susurrat, sed Marcus et Iulia ferociter procedunt, animis liberandis intenti.

A sudden wind whispers through the walls, but Marcus and Julia fiercely press on, determined to free the souls.

In angulis, spectra latent observantia. Marcus, indicium ad libertatem quaerens, muro proximo inspicit.

In the corners, the watching spirits hide. Marcus, searching for a clue to freedom, inspects a nearby wall.

"Inscriptio vetusta!" Marcus exclamat, "Hic via ad libertatem esse videtur."

"An ancient inscription!" Marcus exclaims, "This seems to be the way to freedom."

Subito, lumina subita apparent, spectra fugiunt timore perculsa.

Suddenly, unexpected lights appear, and the spirits flee, struck with fear.

"Manete nobiscum," manes rogant, spem in oculis habentes.

"Stay with us," the spirits plead, hope in their eyes.

"Vobiscum manebimus," Marcus affirmat, timore superato, "vobis auxilium feremus."

"We will stay with you," Marcus affirms, having overcome his fear, "we will help you."

Stella cadens, signum spei, in caelo micat. Marcus et Iulia, una mente, ad novam fortitudinem et spem tendunt.

A falling star, a sign of hope, shines in the sky. Marcus and Julia, united in mind, move toward new strength and hope.

In Umbra Historiae

Nocte constituta, Marcus et Iulia, animos aequos gerentes, Colosseum antiquum explorant. Subito, in tenebris, librum antiquum reperiunt, qui historiam manium continet.

On the appointed night, Marcus and Julia, with calm spirits, explore the ancient Colosseum. Suddenly, in the darkness, they find an ancient book that contains the history of the spirits.

"Ecce!" Marcus exclamat, "Liber antiquus! Fortasse nobis narrationem manium praebebit."

"Look!" Marcus exclaims, "An ancient book! Perhaps it will tell us the story of the spirits."

Iulia librum aperit; imagines spectrorum in paginis apparent. "Horrendum!" susurrat, "Visus terribilis!"

Julia opens the book; images of ghosts appear on the pages. "Horrifying!" she whispers, "A terrible sight!"

Manes per librum legere incipiunt, dolorem et iram suam narrantes. Marcus et Iulia, increduli, mirantur et audiunt.

The spirits begin to speak through the book, narrating their pain and anger. Marcus and Julia, incredulous, are amazed and listen.

"Nocte media," Marcus observat, "lumina et voces per locum resonant. Fortasse ritus antiquus manes liberare potest."

"At midnight," Marcus observes, "lights and voices resonate through the place. Perhaps an ancient ritual can free the spirits."

Sed res necessarias quaerere periculosum est. "Umbrae cum vento moventur," Iulia metuens dicit, "et murmura antiqua audiri possunt."

But seeking the necessary items is dangerous. "The shadows move with the wind," Julia says fearfully, "and ancient murmurs can be heard."

Sub terra, sub Colosseo, locus secretus ritum perficere potest. Marcus et Iulia, signa magica quaerentes, circulum et stellas inveniunt.

Beneath the ground, under the Colosseum, a secret place can complete the ritual. Marcus and Julia, searching for magical signs, find a circle and stars.

"Manes ad circulum veniant," Marcus spem concipit, "verba potentia eos liberare possint."

"Let the spirits come to the circle," Marcus hopes, "perhaps powerful words can free them."

Verbis potentibus pronuntiatis, caelum et terra respondent. "Energia obscura," Marcus dicit, "manes convocat."

As powerful words are spoken, heaven and earth respond. "Dark energy," Marcus says, "is calling the spirits."

Liberatio prope est, manes exspectant, et subito lux subita omnia illuminat, silentium post clamorem super terram imponens.

Freedom is near, the spirits wait, and suddenly a bright light illuminates everything, imposing silence over the land after a great cry.

Marcus et Iulia, gratias agentes, gaudent libertate manium et silentio.

Marcus and Julia, giving thanks, rejoice in the freedom of the spirits and the peace that follows.

Via ad Libertatem

Ritus, inceptus, subito interruptus est. "Periculum adest," Marcus susurrat, "creaturae nocturnae manes perturbant."

The ritual, once started, was suddenly interrupted. "Danger is near," Marcus whispers, "night creatures are disturbing the spirits."

Iulia, firmiter loquens, ait: "Constantes maneamus et ritum perficere conemur. Manes nobis fortasse adiuvare poterunt."

Julia, speaking firmly, says: "Let us stay resolute and try to complete the ritual. The spirits may be able to help us."

Manes, sua fortitudine colligentes, adiuvant. "Verba antiqua resonant," Marcus inquit, "potentia crescens est."

The spirits, gathering their strength, help. "The ancient words are resonating," Marcus says, "the power is growing."

Terra tremit, manes clamant. "Libertatem petimus," Iulia alta voce profert.

The earth trembles, the spirits cry out. "We seek freedom," Julia proclaims loudly.

Subito, umbrae dissolvuntur, lumen clarum apparet. "Silentium subitum," Marcus exclamat, "creaturae fugiunt!"

Suddenly, the shadows dissolve, and a bright light appears. "Sudden silence," Marcus exclaims, "the creatures are fleeing!"

Manes, veram formam ostendentes, pulchritudinem et dolorem simul monstrant. "Gratias vobis agimus," Iulia laeta dicit, "gratiam vobis debemus."

The spirits, showing their true form, reveal both beauty and sorrow. "We thank you," Julia says joyfully, "we owe you our gratitude."

Circulus lucis portam ad aethera efficit. "Ultimum vale," Marcus manibus ad caelum elevatis dicit, "pacem vobis petimus."

A circle of light forms a gateway to the heavens. "A final farewell," Marcus says, raising his hands to the sky, "we wish you peace."

Liberatio completa est, stellae micant. Marcus et Iulia, soli inter monumenta, memoriam manium mente tenent.

The liberation is complete, stars shine brightly. Marcus and Julia, alone among the monuments, hold the memory of the spirits in their minds.

Memoria Aeterna

Post ritum, pax in Colosseo regnat. Marcus et Iulia, labores suos prosequentes, manium memoriam semper conservant.

After the ritual, peace reigns in the Colosseum. Marcus and Julia, continuing their work, always preserve the memory of the spirits.

"Sole orto," Marcus affirmat, "nova dies, nova vita. Sed memoria noctis mirabilis semper nobiscum manebit."

"With the rising sun," Marcus declares, "a new day, a new life. But the memory of that marvelous night will always stay with us."

Iulia ridens addit: "Narratio de nocte illa amicis tradenda est. Imagines et soni in memoria nostra tenaci permanebunt."

Julia, laughing, adds: "The story of that night must be told to friends. The images and sounds will remain in our lasting memory."

Colosseum, non solum locus sed etiam temporum testis, memoriae custos, in animis eorum remanebit.

The Colosseum, not just a place but a witness of times, a keeper of memory, will remain in their minds.

"Manes numquam obliviscemur," Marcus solemniter promittit, "sacrificium eorum numquam inane erit."

"We will never forget the spirits," Marcus solemnly promises, "their sacrifice will never be in vain."

"Spectra amissa," Iulia graviter dicit, "sed memoria aeterna manebit. Liber antiquus, secretorum custos, nobis in perpetuum erit."

"The ghosts are gone," Julia says gravely, "but the eternal memory will remain. The ancient book, keeper of secrets, will be with us forever."

Signum manium, amicitiae aeternae, inter duos iuvenes in corde resonat.

The sign of the spirits, of eternal friendship, echoes in the hearts of the two young ones.

Subito, novi peregrinatores, somnia de manibus audientes, ad Colosseum accedunt. Nox tranquilla, sed historia loquitur.

Suddenly, new travelers, having heard the tales of the spirits, approach the Colosseum. The night is calm, but history speaks.

"Manes liberati," Marcus ad eos narrat, "sed semper praesentes. Colosseum, temporum testis, memoriae custos."

"The spirits are freed," Marcus tells them, "but always present. The Colosseum, a witness of time, a keeper of memory."

Luna plena, nova lux, spiritus liber, inter antiqua monumenta et memorabilem historiam, aeternam quietem promittit.

The full moon, a new light, and a free spirit, among ancient monuments and memorable history, promise eternal peace.

Silvae Umbraeque Aeternae

Fuga Incipit

In silva magna et obscura, septem legionarii Romani ambulant. Post magnum proelium contra Boudiccam, rebellium reginam, fugiunt. Silva densa est et plena tenebrarum.

In a great and dark forest, seven Roman legionaries walk. After a great battle against Boudicca, the rebel queen, they are fleeing. The forest is dense and full of shadows.

Marcus, dux legionariorum, dicit: "Celeriter, amici! Boudicca nos persequitur. In hac silva nos occultare oportet."

Marcus, the leader of the legionaries, says: "Quickly, friends! Boudicca is pursuing us. We must hide in this forest."

Sed subito, natura videtur mutare. Aura frigida eos tangit. Lucius, legionarius, tremens, interrogat: "Sensistine hoc? Silva haec... alia videtur."

But suddenly, nature seems to change. A cold breeze touches them. Lucius, a legionary, trembling, asks: "Did you feel that? This forest... seems different."

In caelo, sol absconditur, et nebula densa apparet. "Quid faciemus?" susurrat Titus, alius legionarius. Omnes circumspiciunt, sed iter apertum non est.

In the sky, the sun hides, and a dense fog appears. "What will we do?" whispers Titus, another legionary. They all look around, but there is no clear path.

Nocte, castra parva constituunt. Ignem faciunt, sed somnia terribilia habent. "Non possum dormire," Gaius, vigilans, susurrat. "Umbrae... circumstant."

At night, they set up a small camp. They make a fire, but have terrible dreams. "I can't sleep," Gaius, keeping watch, whispers. "Shadows... are all around."

Cum prima luce, Marcus statuit: "Profundius in silvam ire oportet. Fortasse exitum inveniemus." Sed silva fit densior et obscurior. Animalia quiescunt; solum venti sonum audiunt.

At first light, Marcus decides: "We must go deeper into the forest. Perhaps we will find a way out." But the forest becomes denser and darker. The animals fall silent; they hear only the sound of the wind.

"Aliquid... hic est," Flavius murmurat. "Non soli sumus." Silva plena mysteriis est. Legionarii sentiunt se non solos esse, sed quid vel quis cum eis sit, ignoratur.

"Something... is here," Flavius murmurs. "We are not alone." The forest is full of mysteries. The legionaries feel they are not alone, but what or who is with them remains unknown.

Spiritus Primi

Iter per silvam densam et obscuram legionarii continuant, sed iter certum invenire non possunt. Subito, in aere clamor terribilis resonat. "Decime! Ubi es?" Marcus clamat, sed nullus respondet.

The legionaries continue their journey through the dense and dark forest, but they cannot find a clear path. Suddenly, a terrible shout echoes in the air. "Decimus! Where are you?" Marcus shouts, but no one responds.

"Vestigia eius sequamur!" Titus proponit. Sed in circulis ambulant, ad eundem locum semper redeuntes. "Quomodo hoc fieri potest?" Lucius confusus murmurat.

"Let's follow his tracks!" Titus suggests. But they walk in circles, always returning to the same place. "How can this be happening?" Lucius murmurs, confused.

Silva densior et obscurior fit, frigusque intensius sentiunt. In tenebris, arborum facies terribiles formantur. "Hoc videte!" Gaius exclamat, sonum ossium audiens.

The forest becomes denser and darker, and they feel the cold growing stronger. In the darkness, terrifying faces are formed in the trees. "Look at this!" Gaius exclaims, hearing the sound of bones.

Ventus incipit susurrare, nomen uniuscuiusque eorum vocans. "Quis nos vocat?" Flavius tremens interrogat. Et subito, spectra pallida inter arbores apparere incipiunt.

The wind begins to whisper, calling each of their names. "Who is calling us?" Flavius asks, trembling. And suddenly, pale ghosts begin to appear among the trees.

Decimus tandem inventus est, sed vultu pallido et oculis vacuis. "Vidi eos... spiritus," susurrat, horribiles fabulas narrans.

Decimus is finally found, but with a pale face and vacant eyes. "I saw them... spirits," he whispers, telling horrible tales.

Nocte, somnia terribilia patiuntur, de morte et perditione. Unus spiritus manifestus fit, Decimum iterum terrens. "Fugere oportet!" Decimus clamat.

At night, they suffer terrible dreams of death and destruction. One spirit becomes visible, terrifying Decimus again. "We must flee!" Decimus shouts.

Sed cum fugere conantur, ad sua castra redeunt, quasi silva eos in laqueum duxisset. Nocte, silentium terribile est, et obscuri spiritus circumvolant.

But when they try to flee, they return to their camp, as if the forest had trapped them. At night, the silence is terrifying, and dark spirits fly around.

"Quid faciemus?" Marcus interrogat, ceteros ad consilium vocans. "Hic manere non possumus. Sed quo ibimus?"

"What will we do?" Marcus asks, calling the others for advice. "We cannot stay here. But where will we go?"

Omnes circum ignem stantes, de futuro incerto cogitant. Silva eos tenet, spiritusque incipiunt ludere.

All standing around the fire, they think about the uncertain future. The forest holds them, and the spirits begin to play with them.

Obsessio

Mane, cum sol oritur, animi legionariorum perturbati sunt. "Aqua nostra paene consumpta est," Titus dicit, utres inspiciens. "Solum pauca frusta panis habemus," Lucius addit, cibum ostendens. Marcus, dux, frontem corrugat. "De futuro timeo," confitetur.

In the morning, as the sun rises, the spirits of the legionaries are troubled. "Our water is almost gone," Titus says, inspecting the flasks. "We only have a few pieces of bread left," Lucius adds, showing the food. Marcus, the leader, furrows his brow. "I fear for the future," he admits.

They wander in the deep forest, unable to find any way out. Suddenly, voices and moans begin to be heard. "Who is there?" Decimus shouts, but no one responds. Shadows and terrifying shapes appear between the trees. "What is that?" Gaius cries, but he suddenly flees from the terrifying sight and does not return.

"Someone touched me!" Flavius exclaims, looking around. "But... no one is here." "At night, our fires go out," Marcus observes. "It's as if the forest itself wants to drive us away."

They walk in circles, always returning to the same place. "Haven't we seen this before?" Lucius asks, confused. They find old stone statues, horrible to look at. "Who placed these?" Titus whispers.

At night, the sounds of distant battle and shouts can be heard. "Do you hear that?" Decimus says, trembling. "It's as if battles are being fought here." Marcus, staying calm, suggests, "We need to communicate with these spirits. Perhaps they can make peace with us."

Sed cum spiritibus loqui conantur, nullus responsum dat. "Cur nos non audiunt?" Lucius dicit, desperatus. Silva viva esse videtur, eorumque motus et voces observans. "Hic manere non possumus," Marcus statuit. "Aliquam viam exire debemus."

But when they try to speak to the spirits, no answer comes. "Why don't they hear us?" Lucius says, desperate. The forest seems alive, observing their movements and voices. "We cannot stay here," Marcus decides. "We must find some way to leave."

Sed quomodo? Silvae umbrae eos tenent, et nulla via exitus apparet. Incipit vera obsessio.

But how? The shadows of the forest hold them, and no way out appears. A true obsession begins.

Voces Mortuorum

Mane, cum primum sol oritur, legionarii ex gravi somno surgunt. "Audisne?" Marcus susurrat. "Voces mortuorum nos vocant." Circumspiciunt, sed nemo praeter ipsos in silva videtur. Folia arborum suaviter moventur, eorumque nomina susurrant. "Quid a nobis volunt?" Titus tremens interrogat.

At dawn, when the first sun rises, the legionaries wake from a heavy sleep. "Do you hear that?" Marcus whispers. "The voices of the dead are calling us." They look around, but no one besides them is seen in the forest. The leaves of the trees gently move, whispering their names. "What do they want from us?" Titus asks, trembling.

Subito, Decimus, pallens, stat. "Vidi eos... mortuos meos. Me vocant," voce fracta dicit. Tenebrae circa eos densescunt, lucem diei obumbrantes. Spectra antiquorum silvae habitantium inter arbores lente moventur, eos sequentes. "Cur nos sequuntur?" Lucius murmurat.

Suddenly, Decimus, pale, stands. "I saw them... my dead. They are calling me," he says in a broken voice. Darkness thickens around them, overshadowing the daylight. The specters of ancient forest dwellers slowly move between the trees, following them. "Why are they following us?" Lucius murmurs.

Cibus reliquus coram eis putrescit, aquaque in utribus amara fit. "Quid hoc est?" Gaius exclamat, cibum proiciens. In terra, signa arcana et symbola repente apparent. "Hoc intellegere non possum," Flavius dicit, terram inspiciens.

The remaining food before them rots, and the water in their flasks turns bitter. "What is this?" Gaius exclaims, throwing the food away. On the ground, arcane signs and symbols suddenly appear. "I cannot understand this," Flavius says, inspecting the ground.

Lucius subito clamat et in silvam currit. Cum inveniunt eum, oculi eius vacui sunt, loqui non potest. "Quid vidisti?" Marcus interrogat, sed Lucius solum tacet. Nocte, somnia legionariorum peiora fiunt, mortem suam praemonstrantia. "Horribile somnium habui," Titus suspirat. "Nos omnes mortui eramus."

Lucius suddenly screams and runs into the forest. When they find him, his eyes are vacant, and he cannot speak. "What did you see?" Marcus asks, but Lucius remains silent. At night, the legionaries' dreams grow worse, foretelling their deaths. "I had a horrible dream," Titus sighs. "We were all dead."

In silva, lignum aridum in formam serpentis mutat. Cum tangere conantur, in pulverem vertitur. "Magia!" Gaius exclamat. Nebulae circa eos densantur, formam hominum assumunt. Sed cum tangere eos conantur, nebulae dissipantur. "Quis hic est?" Decimus dicit, circumspiciens.

In the forest, dry wood turns into the shape of a serpent. When they try to touch it, it crumbles into dust. "Magic!" Gaius exclaims. Mists thicken around them, taking the form of people. But when they try to touch them, the mists dissipate. "Who is here?" Decimus says, looking around.

Apparent spiritus veterum legionariorum Romanorum, tristes et silentes. "Fratres nostri..." Marcus susurrat, spiritus observans. In cortice arborum, vultus formantur, eos directe observantes. "Nos vident," Flavius dicit, retrocedens.

The spirits of ancient Roman legionaries appear, sad and silent. "Our brothers..." Marcus whispers, watching the spirits. Faces form in the bark of the trees, watching them directly. "They see us," Flavius says, stepping back.

Nocte, tota silva videtur susurrare, nomina eorum vocans. "Marcus... Titus... Gaius..." ventus fert. "Hoc loco manere periculosum est," Marcus statuit. "Sed quo ibimus?" Via fugae non est certa. Spiritus mortuorum, spectra, et umbrae silvae eos undique circumdant.

At night, the whole forest seems to whisper, calling their names. "Marcus... Titus... Gaius..." the wind carries. "It is dangerous to stay in this place," Marcus decides. "But where will we go?" The path to escape is uncertain. The spirits of the dead, specters, and shadows of the forest surround them on all sides.

Maledictio Silvae

Legionarii, causam maledictionis explorantes, veteres ruinas in silva inveniunt. "Quid hoc est?" Marcus inquit, ruinas inspectans.

The legionaries, exploring the cause of the curse, find ancient ruins in the forest. "What is this?" Marcus asks, inspecting the ruins.

Altare vetus in medio ruinarum stat, ossibus circumspersis. "Incantationes... audisne?" Flavius susurrat, voces magicas audiens.

An old altar stands in the middle of the ruins, surrounded by bones. "Incantations... do you hear them?" Flavius whispers, hearing magical voices.

Circum altare, spiritus irati apparent. "Sacrificium volunt," Gaius timide dicit. Unus ex legionariis, mente perturbata, ad altare procedit et subito evanescit.

Around the altar, angry spirits appear. "They want a sacrifice," Gaius says fearfully. One of the legionaries, disturbed in mind, approaches the altar and suddenly disappears.

"Solum vestigia eius videre possumus!" Titus exclamat, in terra scripta sanguine ostendens. Rami arborum quasi manus ad eos extenduntur.

"We can only see his footprints!" Titus exclaims, pointing to writing in blood on the ground. The branches of the trees stretch toward them like hands.

Subito, terra sub pedibus eorum movetur, fossaeque apparent. "Adiuvate!" Decimus clamat, sed ceteri eum liberare non possunt.

Suddenly, the ground moves beneath their feet, and pits appear. "Help!" Decimus shouts, but the others cannot free him.

Animalia nocturna, oculis fulgentibus, eos circumdant. "Nos observant... sed cur non appropinquant?" Lucius murmurat.

Nocturnal animals, with glowing eyes, surround them. "They are watching us... but why don't they approach?" Lucius murmurs.

Ad fontem aquae procedunt, sed aqua in sanguinem convertitur. "Hoc bibere non possumus!" Marcus dicit, repudians.

They go to a water spring, but the water turns to blood. "We cannot drink this!" Marcus says, rejecting it.

Umbrae in silva densantur, et lumen lunae vix penetrat. Frigus intensum fit, ignem accendere difficilius est. "Calorem sentire non possum," Flavius tremens inquit.

The shadows in the forest thicken, and the light of the moon barely penetrates. The cold becomes intense, and it is harder to light a fire. "I can't feel the heat," Flavius says, trembling.

Desperati, legionarii se in silva perditi esse sentiunt. "Iter fugae non video," Gaius confitetur, circumspiciens.

Desperate, the legionaries feel lost in the forest. "I don't see a way out," Gaius confesses, looking around.

Nocte, spiritus antecessorum suorum apparere incipiunt, eos monentes. "Exitus non est," spiritus dicunt. "Hic manere oportet."

At night, the spirits of their ancestors begin to appear, warning them. "There is no exit," the spirits say. "You must stay here."

Legionarii, in circulo stantes, de fato suo cogitant. "Quid faciemus?" Titus dicit. "Nonne ullam spem habemus?"

The legionaries, standing in a circle, think about their fate. "What will we do?" Titus says. "Do we have any hope?"

Marcus, ad ceteros conversus, "Fortasse... fortasse aliquid in his ruinis invenire possumus quod nobis adiuvet," proponit. "Explorare oportet."

Marcus, turning to the others, says, "Perhaps... perhaps we can find something in these ruins that can help us. We must explore."

Sed maledictio silvae profundior et obscurior quam credunt est. Omnes vias explorant, sed solutio non facile invenitur. Spiritus silvae, antiqui et potentes, non facile pacantur.

But the curse of the forest is deeper and darker than they believe. They explore all paths, but the solution is not easily found. The spirits of the forest, ancient and powerful, are not easily appeased.

Obsidio Tenebrarum

Ante meridiem, obscuritas subito venit, solque obscuratur. "Quid hoc est?" Lucius exclamat, circumspiciens.

Before midday, darkness suddenly falls, and the sun is obscured. "What is this?" Lucius exclaims, looking around.

Marcus, fortis et constans, "In circulum defendendi nos constituamus. Spirituum impetum exspectemus," iubet, arma tenens.

Marcus, strong and steadfast, commands, "Let us form a defensive circle. Let us prepare for the attack of the spirits," while holding his weapon.

Soni bellorum circum eos resonant, terrorem augentes. "Romani cum Britannis pugnant," Flavius susurrat, oculos in nebula fixos tenens.

The sounds of battles echo around them, increasing their fear. "Romans are fighting with the Britons," Flavius whispers, his eyes fixed on the mist.

Subito, imago pugnae inter Romanos et Britannos in nebula apparet. "Hic locus belli antiqui est," Gaius dicit, spectans intentus pugnam.

Suddenly, an image of the battle between Romans and Britons appears in the mist. "This is the site of an ancient battle," Gaius says, watching the fight intently.

Unus ex legionariis, oculis fascinatus, in imaginem pugnae trahitur. "Lucius!" Marcus clamat, sed Lucius non audet retrospicere.

One of the legionaries, fascinated by the sight, is drawn into the image of the battle. "Lucius!" Marcus shouts, but Lucius dares not look back.

Reliqui quattuor legionarii se solos esse sentiunt. "Umbrae... amicorum nostrorum," Titus tristiter susurrat, formas amicorum suorum videns.

The remaining four legionaries feel utterly alone. "The shadows... of our friends," Titus whispers sadly, seeing the forms of their fallen comrades.

Venti lamentationes portant, nomina eorum vocantes. "Fratres... nos servate," Decimus dicit, voces mortuorum suorum audiens.

The winds carry lamentations, calling their names. "Brothers... save us," Decimus says, hearing the voices of their dead.

Radices sub terra moveri videntur, tentoria eorum subvertunt. "Fugite!" Flavius clamat, sed terra eos detinet.

The roots under the earth seem to move, overturning their tents. "Run!" Flavius shouts, but the ground holds them in place.

Aquis haustis, visiones horribiles patiuntur. "Hic aqua non est," Marcus dicit, abominatus.

With their water consumed, they suffer terrible visions. "There is no water here," Marcus says in disgust.

Spiritus in vento loqui videntur, finem nuntiantes. "Morimur hic," Lucius dicit, desperatus.

The spirits seem to speak in the wind, announcing the end. "We are going to die here," Lucius says, desperate.

Nox sine luna est, stellae occultantur, tenebris completis. "Nihil videre possum," Gaius dicit, frustratus.

The night is moonless, the stars hidden, and darkness fills everything. "I can't see anything," Gaius says, frustrated.

Frigus glaciale eos invadit, ignes non calescunt. "Calor... ubi est calor?" Titus clamat, tremens.

An icy cold invades them, and the fires give no heat. "The warmth... where is the warmth?" Titus shouts, trembling.

Vox clara in silva resonat, ultimum sacrificium postulans. "Quid postulat?" Flavius pavore commotus interrogat.

A clear voice echoes in the forest, demanding the final sacrifice. "What does it want?" Flavius asks, shaken by fear.

Legionarii deficiunt, unus ex eis desideratus, ab spiritibus abductus. "Lucius... ubi es, Lucius?" Marcus clamat, frustratus et tristis.

The legionaries are weakening, one of them missing, taken by the spirits. "Lucius... where are you, Lucius?" Marcus shouts, frustrated and sorrowful.

Ultimum Proelium

Tres supersunt legionarii, territi et desperati. "Quid faciemus, Marce?" Titus timide interrogat.

Three legionaries remain, terrified and desperate. "What will we do, Marcus?" Titus asks timidly.

Marcus, oculos firmos tenens, "Media nocte consilium capiemus. Pugnare vel mori," constans respondet.

Marcus, keeping his eyes steady, responds firmly, "At midnight, we will decide. Fight or die."

"Arma sumite," Marcus iubet, arma scutaque parans. "Tempus pugnandi nunc est."

"Take up your weapons," Marcus commands, preparing his arms and shields. "The time to fight is now."

Spectra densa circum eos congregantur, ultimam pugnam exspectantia. "Nos sequuntur," Gaius murmurat, gladium manu stringens.

Thick specters gather around them, awaiting the final battle. "They are following us," Gaius murmurs, gripping his sword.

Subito, unus legionariorum somnio monetur, exitum per sacrificium praebendum ostenditur. "Sacerdos antiquus... vosmet ipsos sacrificare debetis," voces somni dicunt.

Suddenly, one of the legionaries is warned in a dream, showing that the way out requires a sacrifice. "An ancient priest... you must sacrifice yourselves," the voices of the dream say.

Nihilominus, in pugnam ineunt, umbras ferientes. "Adversus!" Marcus clamat, ferociter pugnans.

Nevertheless, they enter the fight, striking at shadows. "Fight back!" Marcus shouts, fighting fiercely.

Omnia arma inutilia sunt, gladii per auras inanes feriunt. "Nonne hic finis est?" Flavius fatigatus clamat, collabens.

All their weapons are useless, their swords striking through empty air. "Is this not the end?" Flavius, exhausted, cries out, collapsing.

Spiritus maior apparet, gigantis formam gerens. "Adiuvate... adiuvate!" Titus timide invocat.

A greater spirit appears, taking the form of a giant. "Help... help!" Titus timidly calls out.

Terra movetur, arbores evertuntur, legionarii ad fugam versi sunt. "Fugiendum est!" Gaius clamat, terrore constrictus.

The earth shakes, trees are uprooted, and the legionaries turn to flee. "We must run!" Gaius shouts, gripped by terror.

Duo cadunt, terrae motu consumpti. "Amici... valete," Marcus suspirat, animo tristi.

Two fall, consumed by the movement of the earth. "Friends... farewell," Marcus sighs, with a heavy heart.

Ultimus stans, sacerdotem antiquum invocat, auxilium petit. "Nunc... auxilium... precor," inquit Lucius, ad altare procedens.

The last one standing, Lucius, invokes the ancient priest and asks for help. "Now... help... I beg," he says, approaching the altar.

Sacrificium offert, sanguinem suum in terram fundens. "Hic finis est," Lucius tristis dicit.

He offers the sacrifice, pouring his blood into the ground. "This is the end," Lucius says sadly.

Spiritus quiescunt, sed tantum pro momento. "Pax," Marcus susurrat, oculos claudens.

The spirits rest, but only for a moment. "Peace," Marcus whispers, closing his eyes.

Vis maior eum rapit, ad altare trahitur. "Ultimum sacrificium..." Marcus murmurat, in tenebras consumptus.

A greater force takes him, dragging him to the altar. "The final sacrifice..." Marcus murmurs, consumed by darkness.

Ante finem, visionem pacis videt, sed in tenebris consumitur. "Vale... mundo," Marcus dicit, animo resignato.

Before the end, he sees a vision of peace, but he is consumed by the darkness. "Farewell... world," Marcus says, with a resigned heart.

Silentium Aeternum

Ultimus legionarius, solus in silva, morti proximus ambulat. "Ubi sum?" Marcus murmurat, oculos in tenebras fixos tenens.

The last legionary, alone in the forest, walks close to death. "Where am I?" Marcus murmurs, his eyes fixed on the darkness.

Sine ulla directione ambulat, omni spe amissa. "Hic... finis est," fatigatus Titus susurrat.

He walks without direction, all hope lost. "This... is the end," Titus whispers, exhausted.

Spiritus in tenebris congregantur, ultimum sacrificium praeparantes. "Tempus est," Gaius dicit, circulum magicum delineans.

The spirits gather in the darkness, preparing the final sacrifice. "It is time," Gaius says, drawing a magic circle.

Legionarius, in medio circuli stans, finem exspectat. "Nunc... veni," Marcus dicit, voce tremula.

The legionary, standing in the middle of the circle, awaits the end. "Now... come," Marcus says, his voice trembling.

Voces antecessorum audit, consilium et solacium ferentes. "Fortis esse... oportet," Flavius tristiter susurrat.

He hears the voices of his ancestors, bringing counsel and comfort. "You must... be strong," Flavius whispers sadly.

Spiritus antiqui se revelant, silvae historiam narrantes. "Maledictio manet," Decimus voce gravi enuntiat.

The ancient spirits reveal themselves, narrating the history of the forest. "The curse remains," Decimus announces gravely.

Ultimo sacrificio peracto, spiritus pacare conantur. "Sic finis esto," inquit Lucius, sanguinem fundens in terram.

With the final sacrifice completed, the spirits attempt to bring peace. "Let this be the end," Lucius says, pouring his blood onto the ground.

In supremo momento, lumen mirabile apparet. "Quid hoc est?" Marcus exclamat, oculos ad lucem vertens.

In the final moment, a miraculous light appears. "What is this?" Marcus exclaims, turning his eyes to the light.

Pacem internam sentit, quamvis tenebrae mox praevaleant. "Pax... tandem," Titus serenitate plenus susurrat.

He feels inner peace, although the darkness soon prevails. "Peace... at last," Titus whispers, full of serenity.

Arborum rami eum leniter tangunt, quasi finem demonstrantes. "Venite... amici," Marcus ad arborem procedit.

The branches of the trees gently touch him, as if showing him the end. "Come... friends," Marcus says, walking toward the tree.

Visiones vitae ante oculos eius transeunt. "Memoria... aeterna," dicit Flavius, ultimam pacem inveniens.

Visions of his life pass before his eyes. "Eternal... memory," Flavius says, finding his final peace.

Spiritus cum eo colloquuntur, finem doloris nuntiantes. "Valete... fratres," dicit Decimus, spiritus secum ducens.

The spirits speak with him, announcing the end of pain. "Farewell... brothers," Decimus says, leading the spirits with him.

Exspirans, spiritus eum ad lucem ducunt. "Pax... aeterna," Lucius animo tranquillo susurrat.

As he breathes his last, the spirits lead him to the light. "Eternal... peace," Lucius whispers with a calm heart.

Silvae maledictio perseverat, alios exspectans. "Hic... finis non est," Marcus dicit, memoria in aeternum permanens.

The forest's curse endures, waiting for others. "This... is not the end," Marcus says, his memory remaining forever.

Silvae silentium renovatur, memoria legionariorum in aeternum servata. "Pax... in aeternum," Marcus dicit, ultimam requiem inveniens.

The silence of the forest is restored, the memory of the legionaries preserved forever. "Peace... forever," Marcus says, finding his final rest.

Ludi Spectri Aurei

Spectra Domus Aureae

In magnifica Domu Aurea Nero, imperator Romanus, habitat, loco secretorum pleno. Nocte quadam, cum silentium palatium impleverat, Nero, solus in cubiculis suis, sonos inusitatos audit. Tenuem risum puerilem audit, quod viventi homini attribui non potest. Mirans et voce trepida in tenebras clamat: "Quis est hic?"

In the magnificent Golden House, Nero, the Roman emperor, resides, a place full of secrets. One night, when silence had filled the palace, Nero, alone in his chambers, hears unusual sounds. He hears a faint childish laugh, which cannot be attributed to any living person. Wondering and with a trembling voice, he calls out into the darkness: "Who is here?"

Nulla responsio fit, nisi ventus qui per apertas fenestras suaviter susurrat, candelas subito exstinguens. Nero cibum de mensa evanescere observat, et statuae quasi vivae capita movere videntur. Cor eius palpitat, sed curiositas timorem superat.

There is no response, except for the wind softly whispering through the open windows, suddenly extinguishing the candles. Nero observes food disappearing from the table, and the statues seem to move their heads as if they were alive. His heart races, but curiosity overcomes fear.

Ad servos conversus, qui nihil mali viderant, Nero interrogat: "Somnia sunt? An haec omnia vera?" Servi, confusi, solum capita nutant. Nocte illa, Nero fabulam pueri spectri reminiscitur, pueri qui in palatio ludis delectabatur. "Forte," cogitat Nero, "ludum huius spectri investigare oportet."

Turning to the servants, who had seen nothing amiss, Nero asks: "Are these dreams? Or is all of this real?" The servants, confused, only nod their heads. That night, Nero recalls the tale of a ghostly boy who delighted in games within the palace. "Perhaps," Nero thinks, "I should investigate this spirit's game."

Per tacita atria ambulans, risum pueri ad cubiculum vetus sequitur, ubi risus clarior est. Audacia plenus, Nero portam aperit, sed cubiculum vacuum invenit. "Ubi es, puer?" inquit, sed sola responsio silentium est.

Walking through the silent halls, Nero follows the boy's laughter to an old room where the laughter grows louder. Full of courage, Nero opens the door but finds the room empty. "Where are you, boy?" he asks, but the only response is silence.

Mane, Nero ludos spectri animadvertit. Calcei eius sub lecto absconduntur, aqua balnei frigescit, et vox pueri per aulam resonat. "Hic ludere vult," sibi dicit Nero, speculum inspiciens quod ipsum ridiculum reddit. "Ego quoque ludere volo."

In the morning, Nero notices the spirit's games. His shoes are hidden under the bed, the bathwater turns cold, and the boy's voice echoes through the hall. "He wants to play here," Nero says to

himself, looking into a mirror that makes him appear ridiculous. "I
want to play too."

*Nero dolium mellis in atrio parat, ludum nocturnum indicans.
Nocte insequenti, risus per domum resonat, mel in solo effusum est,
sed nullae vestigia apparent. Nero, risum spectri audiens, magis
magisque ludos eius admiratur.*

Nero prepares a jar of honey in the atrium, indicating a nighttime
game. The following night, laughter echoes through the house,
honey is spilled on the floor, but no footprints appear. Nero,
hearing the spirit's laughter, grows more and more amused by its
games.

*"Me ludis delectare non potes," Nero exclamat, sed intus spectri
ingenium et hilaritatem celebrat. Ad bibliothecam veniens, libellos
per aërem motos invenit et in culina cibum pro spectri ludis parat.
Sed, cum revertitur, cibum iam consumptum invenit.*

"You cannot amuse me with your games," Nero exclaims, but
inwardly he celebrates the spirit's cleverness and humor. Arriving
at the library, he finds books moved through the air and prepares
food in the kitchen for the spirit's games. But when he returns, he
finds the food already eaten.

*Frustratus sed non victus, Nero amicos ad cenam invitat ut de
natura spectri disserant. Magi et vates conveniunt, retia invisibilia
et incantationes parantes. Cum spectrum ad cenam apparet, omnes
praeter Neronem illud cernunt, et cibus iterum evanescit.*

Frustrated but undefeated, Nero invites friends to dinner to
discuss the nature of the spirit. Magicians and soothsayers gather,
preparing invisible nets and incantations. When the spirit appears
at the dinner, everyone but Nero sees it, and the food disappears
again.

*"Vale, o spectre ludorum," Nero post cenam dicit, nuntium in
speculo reperiens qui eum ad ludos sequendos invitat. Cum amicis,
invisibilia vestigia sequuntur, ad hortum ducuntur ubi magnum
spectaculum magicum, spectri manu factum, cernunt.*

"Farewell, O playful spirit," Nero says after dinner, finding a message in the mirror inviting him to follow the games. Along with his friends, they follow invisible tracks, leading to the garden where they witness a grand magical spectacle created by the spirit.

Sic, inter ludos et risus, Nero et spectrum inopinatam amicitiam inveniunt, Domus Aurea non iam solum magnifica sed etiam magica et gaudii plena effecta.

Thus, through games and laughter, Nero and the spirit find an unexpected friendship, and the Golden House becomes not only magnificent but also magical and filled with joy.

Ludi Spectri

Post noctem tranquillam, Nero in Domu Aurea sua vigilat. Aurora adveniente, calceos suos sub lecto absconditos reperit. "Quis hoc fecit?" Nero in cubiculo suo solus inquit. Nulla responsio datur.

After a peaceful night, Nero wakes in his Golden House. As dawn arrives, he finds his shoes hidden under the bed. "Who did this?" Nero asks, alone in his room. No answer is given.

Balneum ingressus, aquam, quae calida esse deberet, frigidam invenit. "Brr! Cur aqua frigida est?" Nero clamat. Deinde, in magna aula, vocem pueri audit, sed puerum videre non potest.

Entering the bath, he finds the water, which should be hot, cold. "Brr! Why is the water cold?" Nero shouts. Then, in the great hall, he hears the voice of a boy, but he cannot see the boy.

Bibliothecam petit, ubi scripta sua mutata invenit. Nova verba legens, Nero ridet. "Spectre, esne hic?" circumspiciens interrogat. Nulla responsio datur, sed Nero togam suam in arbore horti pendere videt. "Quare toga mea in arbore est?" miratur.

He goes to the library, where he finds his writings altered. Reading the new words, Nero laughs. "Spirit, are you here?" he asks, looking around. No answer is given, but Nero sees his toga hanging from a tree in the garden. "Why is my toga in the tree?" he wonders.

Ad speculum accedens, imagines distortas in eo videt. Ridens, "Vis ludere, spectre? Et ego!" Nero exclamat. Dolium mellis in atrio parat et noctem exspectat. Mane, mel effusum in solo invenit, sed nullae vestigiae apparent. Per domum, risus resonare potest.

Approaching the mirror, he sees distorted images in it. Laughing, "Do you want to play, spirit? So do I!" Nero exclaims. He prepares a jar of honey in the atrium and waits for the night. In the morning, he finds the honey spilled on the floor, but no footprints appear. Throughout the house, laughter can be heard.

"Spectre, ludos tuos valde admiror," Nero exclamat. In bibliotheca, spectrum libellos movet; Nero sequitur, ridens. Cibum in culina pro ludis spectri parat, sed, cum revertitur, cibum consumptum iam invenit.

"Spirit, I greatly admire your games," Nero exclaims. In the library, the spirit moves books; Nero follows, laughing. He prepares food in the kitchen for the spirit's games, but when he returns, he finds the food already consumed.

Nero, non iratus sed admiratione plenus, dicit: "O spectre, artifex ludorum es! Quid aliud potes facere?" Ita, per Domum Auream, amicitia inter imperatorem Romanum et ludicrum spectrum crescit, noctibus ludis miris hilaritatibusque plenis.

Nero, not angry but full of admiration, says: "Oh spirit, you are a master of games! What else can you do?" Thus, throughout the Golden House, the friendship between the Roman emperor and the playful spirit grows, with nights full of wondrous games and laughter.

Consilium Neronis

Nero, post noctes spectri ludorum plenas, audax consilium capit. "Captare spectrum in animo habeo," solus in suo cubiculo dicit. Multum cogitans, ad magnam cenam amicos invitat.

Nero, after nights full of the spirit's games, makes a bold decision. "I plan to capture the spirit," he says alone in his room. Thinking deeply, he invites his friends to a grand dinner.

"Ad cenam vos omnes voco," Nero amicis annuntiat, "de mirabilibus spectri narraturus." Amici, gaudio affecti, ad Domum Auream conveniunt.

"I invite you all to dinner," Nero announces to his friends, "to tell you about the wonders of the spirit." His friends, filled with joy, gather at the Golden House.

Convivio parato, magi et vates, sapientes virorum, conveniunt. "Spectrum comprehendere cupimus," magus pronuntiat. Retia invisibilia et carmina magica parant, spectri apparitionem exspectantes.

With the banquet prepared, magicians and seers, wise men, gather. "We wish to capture the spirit," a magician proclaims. They prepare invisible nets and magical spells, awaiting the spirit's appearance.

Cum cena parata est, omnes ad mensam sedent, exspectantes. Subito, cibus de mensa evanescit. "Spectrum!" omnes exclamant, sed spectrum nemo videt. Risus brevis auditur, deinde silentium sequitur.

When the dinner is ready, everyone sits at the table, waiting. Suddenly, the food vanishes from the table. "The spirit!" everyone exclaims, but no one sees the spirit. A brief laugh is heard, followed by silence.

Nero, quamquam frustratus, sed non victus, affirmat: "Non desistam." Constantia eius omnium admirationem excitat.

Nero, though frustrated, but not defeated, declares: "I will not give up." His determination inspires admiration in everyone.

Cena finita, Nero in speculo nuntium reperit: "Ludere vultis? Sequimini me!" dicit. "Agite," Nero amicos incitat, "spectrum nos invitat sequi!"

After the dinner ends, Nero finds a message in the mirror: "Do you want to play? Follow me!" it says. "Come on," Nero urges his friends, "the spirit invites us to follow it!"

Invisibilia vestigia secuti, per domum ad hortum mirandum ducuntur. Ibi ludi antiquorum Romanorum imitantur et spectaculum magicum, spectri manu factum, praebetur.

Following invisible tracks, they are led through the house to a marvelous garden. There, games of the ancient Romans are imitated, and a magical spectacle, created by the spirit's hand, is presented.

Nero et amici, oculis plenis mirabilium, spectaculum admirantur. "Quam mirificum!" Nero exclamat. Spectaculo viso, Nero magis delectari se a spectro sentit, ludorum eius exspectatione plenus.

Nero and his friends, with eyes full of wonder, admire the spectacle. "How marvelous!" Nero exclaims. After seeing the show, Nero feels even more delighted by the spirit, full of anticipation for its games.

"O spectre," Nero dicit, "ludi tui me valde delectant. Spero nos amicos esse futuros." Sic, inter ludos et magiam, Nero et spectrum vinculum novum inveniunt, amicitia inter hominem et spiritum in Domu Aurea augente.

"Oh spirit," Nero says, "your games delight me greatly. I hope we will be friends." Thus, through games and magic, Nero and the spirit find a new bond, as the friendship between man and spirit grows within the Golden House.

In Hortis Domus Aureae

Mane, Nero et spectrum in hortis splendidis Domus Aureae conveniunt. "Hodie in hortis ludere decrevimus!" inquit Nero.

In the morning, Nero and the spirit meet in the splendid gardens of the Golden House. "Today we have decided to play in the gardens!" says Nero.

Ludentes pilam invisibilem, risus et clamores per aëra volitant. "Ubi est pila?" Nero ridens interrogat, cum pila ipsum in capite tangit.

Playing with an invisible ball, laughter and shouts fly through the air. "Where is the ball?" Nero asks, laughing, as the ball taps him on the head.

Circum eos, flores aquam coloratam mirabiliter effundunt, terram coloribus variegatis tingentes. Statuae, tamquam vivae, saltare incipiunt, choreas antiquas exprimentes.

Around them, flowers miraculously pour out colored water, painting the ground with varied hues. Statues, as if alive, begin to dance, performing ancient dances.

"Spectre, risum meum provocas!" Nero exclamat, cum spectrum eum ad novum ludum provocat. Ad piscinam procedunt, ubi certamen navigationis instituunt. "Videamus," dicit Nero, "quis victor erit!" Naviculae parvae, ex foliis artificiose factae, aquae committuntur.

"Spirit, you make me laugh!" Nero exclaims, as the spirit challenges him to a new game. They go to the pool, where they set up a boat race. "Let's see," says Nero, "who will be the winner!" Small boats, skillfully made from leaves, are placed in the water.

Spectrum, peritia navigationis praeditum, facile vincit. Nero, applaudens manu, gaudet. "Optime lusisti, spectre!"

The spirit, endowed with sailing skills, easily wins. Nero, clapping his hands, rejoices. "Well played, spirit!"

Subito, pluvia dulcis, qualis numquam ante fuerat, incipit cadere, terram dulcedine imbuens. Nero et spectrum, sub pluvia ludunt, ante statuas saltantes.

Suddenly, a sweet rain, unlike any before, begins to fall, soaking the ground with sweetness. Nero and the spirit play under the rain, before the dancing statues.

Sub arbore sedentes, spectrum de Roma antiqua narrat. "Quam dilexi Romam," dicit spectrum, "ludos, populum, urbem ipsam..."

Sitting under a tree, the spirit speaks about ancient Rome. "How I loved Rome," the spirit says, "the games, the people, the city itself..."

Nero, curiosus de vita spectri, interrogat: "Quis fuisti?" Spectrum respondet: "Puer Romanus, ludis et libertate amans."

Nero, curious about the spirit's life, asks: "Who were you?" The spirit responds: "A Roman boy, a lover of games and freedom."

"Tibi promitto," Nero affatur, "tibi semper locum in palatio meo fore, amice." Ita, amicitia inter imperatorem et spectrum in hortis floret.

"I promise you," Nero says, "you will always have a place in my palace, my friend." Thus, the friendship between the emperor and the spirit flourishes in the gardens.

Contemplantes solem occidentem, pax et amicitia inter eos confirmantur. Horti Domus Aureae, quondam silentii pleni, nunc risu et fabulis antiquis resonant.

Watching the setting sun, peace and friendship between them are confirmed. The gardens of the Golden House, once full of silence, now echo with laughter and ancient tales.

Spectri Ludi Intensificantur

In Domu Aurea, ludi spectri novas metas attingunt. "Quid hodie parasti nobis, spectre?" Nero, expectatione plenus, interrogat.

In the Golden House, the spirit's games reach new heights. "What have you prepared for us today, spirit?" Nero asks, full of expectation.

Cum prima lux diei affulget, in convivio grande spectaculum lucis et soni exoritur. "Ecce!" Nero exclamat, videns vasa per aëra volitare et musicam ex nihilo ubique resonare.

As the first light of day shines, a grand spectacle of light and sound arises during the feast. "Look!" Nero exclaims, seeing dishes flying through the air and music resonating from nowhere all around.

"Spectre, me ad tectum duc," Nero rogat. Ibi, spectrum stellas nocturnas demonstrat, quasi manu tangi possint. "Quam pulchrae sunt!" Nero susurrat.

"Spirit, take me to the roof," Nero requests. There, the spirit shows him the night stars, as if they could be touched by hand. "How beautiful they are!" Nero whispers.

Per aulam ambulant, et funiculus invisibilis subito eos ad risum provocat. Adhuc mirabilius, sella Neronis in aere levitare incipit. "Magica ars!" Nero exclamat.

They walk through the hall, and an invisible string suddenly makes them burst into laughter. Even more amazing, Nero's chair begins to levitate in the air. "Magic art!" Nero exclaims.

In atrio, nebulae coloratae quasi arcum caelestem creant. In thermis, aqua calida et frigida alternat, Nero ludens in aqua ridet.

In the atrium, colorful mists create a rainbow-like arch. In the baths, hot and cold water alternates, and Nero laughs while playing in the water.

Subito, vestes servorum mirabiliter mutantur, magna confusione creata. "Num tu es, spectre?" Nero ridens inquit. Piscina vino plena invenitur. "Vera festivitas est!"

Suddenly, the servants' clothes are miraculously changed, creating great confusion. "Is this your doing, spirit?" Nero asks, laughing. A pool filled with wine is discovered. "This is a real celebration!"

Signa in parietibus mutare incipiunt, ridiculas fabulas narrantes. "Nunquam scivi parietes fabulas narrare posse!" Nero miratur. In horto, fructus incipiunt loqui. "Salve, Nero!" dicunt.

The paintings on the walls begin to change, telling funny stories. "I never knew walls could tell stories!" Nero marvels. In the garden, the fruit begins to talk. "Hello, Nero!" they say.

Denique, Nero imaginem spectri ex pannis creat, sperans verum spectrum terrere. Cum "terror" spectri apparet, omnes, incluso spectro, in risum prorumpunt.

Finally, Nero creates an image of the spirit out of cloth, hoping to scare the real spirit. When the "ghost" appears, everyone, including the spirit, bursts into laughter.

Die concluso, in speculo figura pueri spectri, risu plena, apparet. "Ludi tui incredibiles sunt," Nero speculo alloquens dicit. "Cras iterum ludamus!"

At the end of the day, the figure of the ghostly boy, full of laughter, appears in the mirror. "Your games are incredible," Nero says, speaking to the mirror. "Let us play again tomorrow!"

Ita, ludis et cachinnis inter se mixtis, vinculum inter Neronem et spectrum magis confirmatur, Domus Aurea non solum magnifici splendoris sed etiam gaudii ludorumque locum demonstrans.

Thus, with games and laughter intertwined, the bond between Nero and the spirit is further strengthened, showing that the Golden House is not only a place of magnificent splendor but also of joy and games.

Sic, inter risus et magica, amicitia inter Neronem et spectrum confirmatur, Domus Aurea locum laetitiae et mirabilium efficiens.

Thus, between laughter and magic, the friendship between Nero and the spirit is confirmed, making the Golden House a place of joy and wonder.

Nox Mysteriosa

Nocte quadam in Domu Aurea, res insolita evenit. Lucernae sponte, sine ullo tactu, accenduntur, viam per tenebras monstrantes. "Quo ducimur?" Nero interrogat, spectrum sequens, quod pariter curiosum apparet.

One night in the Golden House, something unusual happens. The lamps light up on their own, without being touched, showing a path through the darkness. "Where are we being led?" Nero asks, following the spirit, which also appears curious.

Ad cryptam secretam, diu neglectam, perveniunt. "Thesaurus!" Nero exclamat, lumine in angulo cryptae conspicato. Manus spectri, lumine clarissimo circumfusa, ad thesaurum demonstrat.

They reach a secret crypt, long neglected. "Treasure!" Nero exclaims, noticing a light in the corner of the crypt. The spirit's hand, surrounded by a brilliant light, points to the treasure.

"Mirabile visu!" Nero confirmat. Ibi, cum spectro, ludum scaenicum agunt, thesaurum celebrantes, cantu risuque antiquo per cryptam resonantes.

"Amazing to see!" Nero confirms. There, with the spirit, they perform a theatrical play, celebrating the treasure, with songs and ancient laughter echoing through the crypt.

Crypta relicta, statuam loquentem inveniunt. Statua, voce aenigmatum plena, eos provocat: "Audite et invenietis," dicit. Aenigma eos per aedes Domus Aureae ad bibliothecam secretam deducit.

Leaving the crypt, they find a talking statue. The statue, with a voice full of riddles, challenges them: "Listen and you will find," it says. The riddle leads them through the halls of the Golden House to a secret library.

In bibliotheca obscura, librum magicum, lumine lucernae illuminatum, inveniunt. "Liber iste," inquit Nero, "historiam spectri et Domus Aureae narrat."

In the dark library, they find a magic book, illuminated by the light of a lamp. "This book," says Nero, "tells the history of the spirit and the Golden House."

Libro lecto, comperiunt spectrum quondam principem puerum fuisse, qui in palatio ludis risuque fruebatur. "Princeps fuisti?" Nero, admiratus, ad spectrum spectans interrogat.

After reading the book, they learn that the spirit was once a princely boy, who enjoyed games and laughter in the palace. "Were you a prince?" Nero, amazed, asks the spirit.

"De tua historia librum conficiam," Nero spondet. Libro aperto, ventus validus libros circumagit, antiquae magiae spirans.

"I will write a book about your story," Nero promises. When the book is opened, a strong wind stirs the books around, breathing ancient magic.

Spectrum, ridens, Neroni artem magicam volandi tradit. "Volare possumus!" Nero exclamat, cum spectro per aedes et hortos volitant, gaudio repleti.

The spirit, laughing, teaches Nero the magic art of flying. "We can fly!" Nero exclaims, as they soar through the halls and gardens with the spirit, filled with joy.

Luna stellisque lucebantibus, risus eorum per noctem effunditur, amicitia inter mortalem et spiritum nocte mysteriosa crescente.

With the moon and stars shining, their laughter spreads through the night, as the friendship between mortal and spirit grows on a mysterious night.

Paratio Convivii Magni

Nero, imperator Romanus, convivium magni momenti in Domu Aurea praeparat. "Hoc convivium," inquit Nero, "in honorem spectri celebrabitur." Nero omnes Romanos nobiles et sapientes ad convivium magni momenti evocat. "Noctem magicam plenamque mirabilium promitto," Nero in epistula scribit.

Nero, the Roman emperor, prepares an important banquet in the Golden House. "This banquet," Nero says, "will be celebrated in honor of the spirit." Nero invites all the Roman nobles and wise men to this important gathering. "I promise a magical night full of wonders," Nero writes in the letter.

Cum spectrum convenit, promittunt: "Illusiones mirabiles creabimus." Gaudio repleti, ad magnum opus se accingunt. Convivium in horto sub luna et stellis instituitur. Mensae magica vi sustentatae cibum potumque omnibus offerunt. Musica, sine ullo musico viso, ubique resonat, saltatoresque aetherii inter convivas volitant.

When Nero meets with the spirit, they promise: "We will create marvelous illusions." Filled with joy, they set to work on the great task. The banquet is held in the garden under the moon and stars. Tables, supported by magic, offer food and drink to everyone. Music, without any visible musicians, echoes everywhere, and ethereal dancers float among the guests.

"Ecce!" exclamat Nero, cum fontes vini et mellis miraculose fluere incipiunt. Omnes spectaculo attoniti sunt, dum spectrum, lumine lunari illustratum, se revelat. Applausus magnus sonat.

"Look!" Nero exclaims, as fountains of wine and honey miraculously begin to flow. Everyone is astonished by the spectacle, while the spirit, illuminated by the moonlight, reveals itself. A great applause follows.

Gestu manu, spectrum caelum nocturnum mutat, novas constellationes creans. In horto, per focos magicos, spectri vitae imagines proiciuntur, eius historiam sine verbis enarrantes. Convivium facibus et laternis festivis mirabiliter clauditur, quae caelum nocturnum splendidis luminibus illuminant. "Quam pulchrum!" omnes exclamant, amicitiam inter Neronem et spectrum celebrantes.

With a gesture of its hand, the spirit changes the night sky, creating new constellations. In the garden, through magical fires, images of the spirit's life are projected, telling its story without words. The banquet ends miraculously with torches and festive lanterns lighting up the night sky with splendid lights. "How beautiful!" everyone exclaims, celebrating the friendship between Nero and the spirit.

Nocte finita, convivae "noctem magicam" celebrant, spectro pro mirabilibus quae viderunt et senserunt gratias agentes. "Gratias tibi, spectre, pro amicitia et magia," Nero, manum spectri tenens, dicit. "Memoria huius convivii semper nobiscum erit," spectrum cum gaudio et gratitudine respondet.

As the night ends, the guests celebrate the "magical night," thanking the spirit for the wonders they saw and felt. "Thank you, spirit, for your friendship and magic," Nero says, holding the spirit's hand. "The memory of this banquet will always be with us," the spirit responds with joy and gratitude.

Ita, amicitia et magia coniunctae, Domus Aurea locum mirabilium et laetitiae efficit, ubi fabulae et historiae vitam inveniunt.

Thus, with friendship and magic combined, the Golden House becomes a place of wonders and joy, where stories and legends come to life.

Pax

Post finem magni convivii, Nero et spectrum in hortis Domus Aureae considunt, caelum nocturnum et stellas contemplantes. "Tibi gratias ago," inquit Nero, "pro amicitia et ludis mirabilibus."

After the end of the great banquet, Nero and the spirit sit in the gardens of the Golden House, contemplating the night sky and stars. "I thank you," says Nero, "for your friendship and marvelous games."

Spectrum, suaviter respondens, dicit: "Et ego tibi gratias ago, Nero. Amore domum meam implevisti."

The spirit, gently replying, says: "And I thank you, Nero. You have filled my home with love."

Manus suas extendunt, amicitiam aeternam spondentes. Subito, lux divina eos circumdat, pacem et felicitatem nuntians.

They extend their hands, pledging eternal friendship. Suddenly, a divine light surrounds them, announcing peace and happiness.

"Spectaculum tibi ostendere volo," spectrum dicit et veram suam formam revelat: princeps Romanus antiquus. "Missus sum ad te," profert, "ut te de vita et risu doceam."

"I want to show you something," the spirit says and reveals its true form: an ancient Roman prince. "I was sent to you," it says, "to teach you about life and laughter."

Maledictio, quae spectrum tenebat, solvitur, et anima eius liberatur. Nero, lacrimis gaudio plenis, "Gratias tibi ago," pronuntiat.

The curse that held the spirit is lifted, and its soul is freed. Nero, with tears of joy, declares, "Thank you."

Spectrum in caelum ascendens "Vale" dicit. Nero, plenus amoris et gratitudinis, in horto monumentum statuit, memoriam spectri conservans.

The spirit, ascending into the sky, says, "Farewell." Filled with love and gratitude, Nero erects a monument in the garden, preserving the spirit's memory.

Pax et hilaritas, quae olim a Domu Aurea aberant, nunc restitutae sunt. Nero, ad monumentum saepe accedens, de amicitia spectri semper cogitat.

Peace and joy, which were once absent from the Golden House, have now been restored. Nero, often approaching the monument, always thinks about the spirit's friendship.

Narratio amicitiae Neronis cum spectro, quae risum amoremque continet, saeculis tradita, memoriam apud Romanos posterosque conservat.

The story of Nero's friendship with the spirit, filled with laughter and love, is passed down through the ages, preserving the memory among Romans and future generations.

Iter Aeliae

In Pompeianis Ruinis

Cum crepusculum in Pompeiis appropinquaret, Aelia, iuvenis femina Romana, pulchra et curiosa, prope antiquas urbis ruinas ambulabat. Historia loci, olim a Vesuvii montis eruptione deleti, eam vehementer commoverat. Dum sol lente occidebat et caelum flammis vespertinis tingebatur, Aelia ruinas venerandas respexit, corde pleno mirationis et desiderii sciendi quid vere accidisset.

As dusk approached in Pompeii, Aelia, a young Roman woman, beautiful and curious, walked near the ancient ruins of the city. The history of the place, once destroyed by the eruption of Mount Vesuvius, had deeply moved her. While the sun slowly set and the sky was tinged with the flames of evening, Aelia looked upon the venerable ruins, her heart full of wonder and the desire to know what had truly happened.

"Vesuvii montis eruptionem memini," Aelia secum cogitabat, voce plena reverentiae. Ruinae, nunc in tranquillo crepusculo iacentes, silentes et desertae videbantur, mysterium priscum et historias non narratas celantes.

"I remember the eruption of Mount Vesuvius," Aelia thought to herself, her voice full of reverence. The ruins, now lying in the calm twilight, seemed silent and deserted, hiding an ancient mystery and untold stories.

Dum ibi stetit, ruinas contemplans, subito ventus spirare et caelum paulatim obscurari coepit, quasi natura ipsa portam ad praeteritum aperire vellet. Tunc, modo mirabili, voce susurrante circumdata est. "Quis est?" Aelia alta voce clamavit, sed nullus respondit.

As she stood there, contemplating the ruins, the wind suddenly began to blow, and the sky gradually darkened, as if nature itself wanted to open a door to the past. Then, in a miraculous way, she was surrounded by a whispering voice. "Who is there?" Aelia shouted loudly, but no one answered.

Repente, sensum frigidi tactus per tergum suum sentit, se convertit, sed nihil praeter crescentes tenebras videt. Cor eius cito pulsat, respiratio eius fit gravior, sed intus in corde suo scit se non solam esse.

Suddenly, she felt the cold touch down her back, she turned, but saw nothing except the growing darkness. Her heart raced, her breathing grew heavier, but deep inside her heart, she knew she was not alone.

"Sine timore sum," Aelia intra se murmuravit. "Quis me vocat?" iterum clamat, sed responsio nulla erat, nisi venti sonus qui nunc quasi voces antiquas susurrare videbatur.

"I am without fear," Aelia murmured to herself. "Who calls me?" she shouted again, but there was no answer, only the sound of the wind, which now seemed to whisper ancient voices.

Tunc, potentia quaedam invisibilis, tamquam manu spectri ducta, eam in ipsas ruinas traxit. Aelia, corde pleno curiositate et modico timore, se repente in profundis ruinis invenit, ubi historia et mysteria nunc explorare poterat.

Then, some invisible force, as if guided by the hand of a ghost, drew her into the very ruins. Aelia, her heart full of curiosity and a bit of fear, suddenly found herself deep within the ruins, where she could now explore history and mysteries.

Et sic incipit Aeliae iter nocturnum, ducta visione et vocibus e praeterito, per ruinas Pompeianas, ubi umbrae antiquae adhuc errare videntur, quae adhuc multa secreta servant.

And so begins Aelia's nocturnal journey, guided by visions and voices from the past, through the ruins of Pompeii, where ancient shadows still seem to wander, keeping many secrets.

Spiritus Incognitus

Aelia, audax et plena curiositatis, in ruinis Pompeianis manere statuit. Nocte obscura, sola luna viam illi monstrat. Ad antiquam domum pervenit, cuius porta mirabiliter aperta est.

Aelia, bold and full of curiosity, decides to remain in the ruins of Pompeii. In the dark night, only the moon shows her the way. She arrives at an ancient house, whose door is miraculously open.

Intrat Aelia, et mox pavimentum sub pedibus eius gemere audit. Domus imaginibus de vita Pompeianorum repletur, tam vividis ac si modo vita excessissent.

Aelia enters, and soon she hears the floor groaning beneath her feet. The house is filled with images of the life of the Pompeians, so vivid as if they had just left.

Subito, Aelia candelabrum videt quod movetur, nullo praesente. "Estne aliquis hic?" magna voce clamat. Sed nullus respondet, nisi cor eius, quod fortiter pulsat. Deinde, suspirium longum et gelidum audit, quod per ossa eius transire videtur.

Suddenly, Aelia sees a candlestick moving, though no one is present. "Is someone here?" she shouts loudly. But no one answers, except her heart, which beats strongly. Then, she hears a long, cold sigh, which seems to pass through her bones.

Stupefacta, ad fenestram se vertit et figuram pallidam conspicit. Sed cum accuratius inspicit, figura velut umbra evanescit. Aelia, corde tremens sed animo captivata, per domum incedit, sequens vestigia umbrae.

Stunned, she turns to the window and sees a pale figure. But when she looks more closely, the figure vanishes like a shadow. Aelia, her heart trembling but her mind captivated, walks through the house, following the traces of the shadow.

In atrio ludibrium pueri antiquum invenit, temporis pristini reliquum. "Cur hic es?" sibi susurrat, ludibrium manu tenens. Miratur quomodo res tam vetus, historia tam diu praeterita, adhuc tangi, sentiri, memoriaque revocari possit.

In the atrium, she finds an ancient child's toy, a remnant of a distant time. "Why are you here?" she whispers to herself, holding the toy in her hand. She marvels at how something so old, from a history long past, can still be touched, felt, and remembered.

Domus silentium profundum servat, praeter venti susurros et sonum propriae respirationis. Aelia, corde pleno audaciae, per tenebras domus movetur, spiritum illum incognitum quaerens qui vocem suam susurravit. Sentit se non solum vestigia historiae secutam esse, sed etiam ad arcana quaedam, fortasse aetatis longinquae, revelanda venisse.

The house keeps a deep silence, except for the whispers of the wind and the sound of her own breathing. Aelia, her heart full of courage, moves through the darkness of the house, seeking that unknown spirit that whispered to her. She feels that she has not only followed the footsteps of history but also arrived at some mysteries, perhaps of a long-ago age, waiting to be revealed.

Noctis Secreta

Aelia, ludibrium pueri tenens, ex antiqua domo exit et in noctem profundam se immergit. Luna plena in caelo alto resplendet, omnia clara luce illuminans. Sed, dum per ruinas ambulat, terra subito tremere incipit. Timet, sed intra se fortitudinem invenit ut pergere possit.

Aelia, holding the child's toy, exits the ancient house and plunges into the deep night. The full moon shines high in the sky, illuminating everything with a bright light. But as she walks through the ruins, the ground suddenly begins to shake. She is afraid, but within herself, she finds the strength to continue.

In tenebris, voces susurrantes audit, sed quae dicant discernere non potest. Statuas antiquas videt, quae in lumine lunae moveri videntur. Cor eius velociter pulsat, terrore magno captum.

In the darkness, she hears whispering voices, but she cannot discern what they are saying. She sees ancient statues, which seem to move in the moonlight. Her heart beats quickly, gripped by great fear.

Subito magnus sonus, quasi fragor tonitruum, per aëra discinditur. Aelia circumspicit, sed nihil praeter noctis umbras videt. Tum, in parietibus antiquis, picturae quasi ad vitam venire incipiunt, fabulas sine verbis narrantes.

Suddenly, a great sound, like the crash of thunder, tears through the air. Aelia looks around but sees nothing except the shadows of the night. Then, on the ancient walls, paintings begin to come to life, telling stories without words.

Una pictura puellam tristem et solam monstrat. Aelia, corde mota, tristitiam profundam puellae in pictura sentit, ac si proprias eius lacrimas sentiret. Cum ad picturam manum extendit, tactu frigido et inexplicabili occurrit.

One painting shows a sad and lonely girl. Aelia, moved in her heart, feels the deep sadness of the girl in the painting, as if she were feeling the girl's tears herself. When she reaches out her hand to the painting, she is met with a cold and inexplicable touch.

Ventus repente surgit, eam fortiter circumdat. In hoc vento tumultuoso, vocem audire videtur, velut susurrum levis brisae: "Me sequere." Aelia, nunc prorsus captivata mysterio noctis, se parat sequi vocem, quamvis nesciat quo eam ducat. Sensit enim se ad aliquid magnum et arcanum vocari, ad secretum noctis quod forte numquam antea revelatum est.

Suddenly, the wind rises and strongly surrounds her. In this turbulent wind, she seems to hear a voice, like the whisper of a gentle breeze: "Follow me." Aelia, now fully captivated by the mystery of the night, prepares to follow the voice, though she does not know where it will lead her. For she felt called to something great and mysterious, to a secret of the night that perhaps had never before been revealed.

Umbrae Praeteritae

Aelia, voce mysteriosa ducta, per vias antiquas et nebulas densas incedit. Nebula visionem eius obscurat, sed interdum figuras humanas quasi spectras videre potest. Voces circum eam clariores fiunt, preces et clamores antiquorum Pompeianorum audit, quorum vultus in nebula celantur.

Aelia, led by the mysterious voice, walks through ancient streets and thick mist. The mist obscures her vision, but occasionally she can see human figures like specters. The voices around her grow clearer, and she hears the prayers and cries of ancient Pompeians, whose faces are hidden in the mist.

Dum per ruinas ambulat, in medio vetustarum aedium, circulus luminis subito apparet. Aelia accedit, manu temere lumen tangit. Frigidum est, sed aliquo modo invitans. Circulus luminis se aperit et, quasi porta in alium mundum, vitam Pompeianam ante Vesuvii eruptionem monstrat.

As she walks through the ruins, suddenly a circle of light appears in the midst of the old buildings. Aelia approaches and hesitantly touches the light. It is cold but somehow inviting. The circle of light opens and, like a door to another world, reveals Pompeian life before the eruption of Vesuvius.

Aelia quotidianam vitam ante oculos efflorescentem miratur: homines in mercatu ambulantes, risus, clamores vendentium. Subito, serenitas in terrorem mutatur. Caelum obscuratur et Vesuvius magna vi erumpit. Clamores terroris et confusio sequuntur. Aelia, licet tantum spectatrix sit, desperationem et timorem eorum profunde sentit.

Aelia marvels as daily life blooms before her eyes: people walking in the market, laughter, the shouts of vendors. Suddenly, the serenity turns into terror. The sky darkens, and Vesuvius erupts with great force. Screams of terror and confusion follow. Though she is only a spectator, Aelia deeply feels their desperation and fear.

Subito, omnia in tenebras merguntur. Lumen clauditur et Aelia iterum in ruinarum silentio sola relinquitur. Sed, in hac obscuritate, aliquid inexpectatum accidit: manus tenera eam tenet. Aelia convertit et puerum videt, oculos magnos timore plenos habentem.

Suddenly, everything plunges into darkness. The light closes, and Aelia is once again left alone in the silence of the ruins. But in this darkness, something unexpected happens: a gentle hand holds her. Aelia turns and sees a boy, his wide eyes full of fear.

"Puer, quis es? Quomodo te adiuvare possum?" Aelia interrogat, voce tremente, sed plena compassionis.

"Boy, who are you? How can I help you?" Aelia asks, her voice trembling but full of compassion.

"Adiuva me," puer susurrat, voce vix audibili. "Perditi sumus, lumen quaerimus."

"Help me," the boy whispers, his voice barely audible. "We are lost, we seek the light."

Aelia, nunc non solum curiosa sed etiam misericordia mota, puerum ducere decernit. Sentit se non solum testem praeteriti esse, sed etiam partem alicuius maioris, missionis cuiusdam ad spiritus antiquos adiuvandos. Haec est nox plena mysteriis et historiae, qua Aelia non solum in Pompeianorum ruinis, sed etiam inter eorum animas perditas et adhuc vagantes immersa est.

Aelia, now moved not only by curiosity but also by compassion, decides to lead the boy. She feels that she is not only a witness to the past but also part of something greater, a mission to help the ancient spirits. This is a night full of mysteries and history, where Aelia finds herself immersed not only in the ruins of the Pompeians but also among their lost and still wandering souls.

Eruptionis Memoriae

Aelia, manu pueri tenens, cum celeritate per ruinas fugit. Sentit gravitatem momenti, desperationem et tristitiam animarum quae per saecula in his ruinis relictae sunt. Sed iam non solum timet; sentit se missionem habere, spiritus ad pacem ducendi.

Aelia, holding the boy's hand, runs swiftly through the ruins. She feels the weight of the moment, the desperation and sadness of the souls that have been left in these ruins for centuries. But now, she is no longer only afraid; she feels she has a mission, to lead the spirits to peace.

Cum ad locum sacrum perveniunt, sub lumine lunae plenae, aliae umbrae ad eos lente accedunt. Aelia, circumdata silentio noctis et umbris spectrorum, incipit orare. Verba antiqua et potentia dicit, spiritus ad requiem vocans.

When they arrive at the sacred place, under the light of the full moon, other shadows slowly approach them. Aelia, surrounded by the silence of the night and the shadows of spirits, begins to pray. She speaks ancient and powerful words, calling the spirits to rest.

Puer, quem ducit, primo timide, deinde confidenter, in circulum luminis ingreditur. Dum hoc facit, circulus luminis clarior et maior fit. Una post aliam, omnes umbrae in lucem gradiuntur, visu pacificae.

The boy she leads, first timidly, then confidently, steps into the circle of light. As he does this, the circle of light becomes brighter and larger. One by one, all the shadows step into the light, appearing peaceful.

Profundum est silentium et sensus pacis per aërem diffunditur. Aelia sola stat, sub lumine lunae, sentiens onus quod portavit levatum esse. Missionem suam completam esse sentit.

There is a profound silence, and a sense of peace spreads through the air. Aelia stands alone, under the moonlight, feeling that the burden she carried has been lifted. She feels that her mission is complete.

Subito, caelum mutatur. Aurora apparet et sol oritur, signum novi diei. Aelia, nunc tranquilla et contenta, sentit se aliquid magni effecisse. Non solum historiam Pompeianorum profunde intellexit, sed etiam animis perditis adiuvandis partem suam contulit.

Suddenly, the sky changes. Dawn appears, and the sun rises, a sign of a new day. Aelia, now calm and content, feels that she has accomplished something great. She has not only deeply understood the history of the Pompeians, but also contributed her part to helping lost souls.

Respiciens ad ruinas in lumine novi diei, Aelia promittit hoc locum numquam oblivisci. Cum primo ad Pompeianas ruinas venit, historiam et mysterium explorare voluit. Nunc, cum novum diem salutat, partem eius historiae et eius mysterii portat.

Looking back at the ruins in the light of the new day, Aelia promises never to forget this place. When she first came to the Pompeian ruins, she wanted to explore their history and mystery. Now, as she greets the new day, she carries with her a part of its history and mystery.

Finito hoc itinere, Aelia non solum de Pompeiis multa didicit, sed etiam de vita, morte, et humanitatis continuitate. Et cum sol altius in caelo ascendit, viam domum capiens, scit verum munus suum—spirituum requiem—completum esse.

With this journey completed, Aelia has not only learned much about Pompeii, but also about life, death, and the continuity of humanity. And as the sun rises higher in the sky, making her way home, she knows that her true task—the rest of the spirits—has been fulfilled.

Saga Veteris Magicae

Conventus Incipit

Nocte quaedam tempestiva, sub caelo tonante et micantibus fulguribus, tres sagae Etruscae, Alba, Bruna, et Cinis nomine, in silva secreta prope antiquam ruinam conveniunt. Locum magicum ad ritum incipiendum parant, circulum magicum delineantes.

On a stormy night, under a sky full of thunder and flashing lightning, three Etruscan witches, named Alba, Bruna, and Cinis, meet in a secret forest near an ancient ruin. They prepare the magical place to begin the ritual, drawing a magic circle.

"Herbas magicas hic ponamus," Alba dicit, lapidesque et herbas in circulo disponunt. Flammas parvas magicas mox incendunt, carmenque incipiunt, voce gravi et mystica cantantes.

"Let's place the magical herbs here," says Alba, and they arrange stones and herbs in the circle. Soon, they ignite small magical flames and begin to chant a song, their voices deep and mystical.

Ventus surgere incipit, folia circumvolitantia agitans. "Nunc, speculum obscurum in medio circuli ponamus," Cinis suadet. Speculum collocant, et manus iungunt, magicae potentiae invocandae causa.

The wind begins to rise, stirring the swirling leaves. "Now, let us place the dark mirror in the middle of the circle," Cinis suggests. They place the mirror and join hands to invoke magical power.

Subito, speculum lucem emittit et novas sedes monstrat. Incertae voces ex speculo audiri incipiunt. Alba forti voce clamat: "Spiritus, venite!" Et terra sub pedibus earum tremit, umbraeque circa circulum lente formantur, mysterium augentes.

Suddenly, the mirror emits light and reveals new visions. Uncertain voices begin to be heard from the mirror. Alba shouts boldly: "Spirits, come!" And the ground trembles beneath their feet, while shadows slowly form around the circle, adding to the mystery.

"Quid videtis?" Bruna susurrat, ad ceteras spectans.

"What do you see?" Bruna whispers, looking at the others.

"Potentiam... et fortasse periculum," Cinis respondet, speculum intenta observans.

"Power... and perhaps danger," Cinis replies, observing the mirror intently.

Et sic, sagarum conventus incipit, plenus magicae potentiae et incertarum consequentiarum, in nocte plena mysterii et arcanorum.

And so, the witches' gathering begins, full of magical power and uncertain consequences, on a night filled with mystery and secrets.

Spiritus Evocati

Umbrae ad speculi lucem cito congregantur. Sagae, timore captivae, tamen cantum non desistunt.

The shadows quickly gather at the light of the mirror. The witches, though gripped by fear, do not stop their chant.

"Formas hominum vident!" Cinis exclamat, umbras mutantes observans.

"They see human shapes!" Cinis exclaims, watching the shifting shadows.

"Sunt... sunt tristes," Bruna addit, voces clariores audiens. Lamenta et gemitus per silvam resonant.

"They are... they are sad," Bruna adds, hearing the voices more clearly. Wails and groans echo through the forest.

Bruna subito cantare cessat, timore magno affecta. "Non possum... nimis terribile est," dicit.

Bruna suddenly stops chanting, overwhelmed by great fear. "I can't... it's too terrifying," she says.

"Fortiores fiunt!" Alba clamat, circulum perturbatum videns. Umbrae magis magisque obscurae fiunt.

"They are getting stronger!" Alba shouts, seeing the circle disturbed. The shadows grow darker and darker.

Cinis, anxietate plena, exclamat: "Desistamus! Periculum est!" Sed iam sero est. Umbra fortissima, figura tenebrosa et immanis, e speculo exit et ad sagas spectat.

Cinis, full of anxiety, exclaims: "Let's stop! It's dangerous!" But it is already too late. The strongest shadow, a dark and immense figure, emerges from the mirror and gazes at the witches.

Territae, sagae retrocedunt. Umbrae, libertate data, circum silvam volitant, ruinam petentes.

Terrified, the witches step back. The shadows, now freed, fly around the forest, heading toward the ruins.

"Spiritum hunc redigere debemus," Alba dicit, consilium capiens. Herbam potentem adfert et flammas obscuras incendit, ritum incipiendum praeparans.

"We must send this spirit back," Alba says, taking action. She brings forth a powerful herb and lights dark flames, preparing to begin the ritual.

Bruna, spem recipiens, symbola magica circum circulum celeriter delineat. "Haec nos protegent," sperat.

Bruna, regaining hope, quickly draws magical symbols around the circle. "These will protect us," she hopes.

"Tum, incipiamus," Cinis dicit, et cantum potentiorem incipit, voce forti et clara. Umbrae, vocatae, ad circulum revertuntur, tumultu et sonitu magno.

"Then let's begin," Cinis says, and starts a more powerful chant, her voice strong and clear. The shadows, called back, return to the circle with great commotion and noise.

Sagae, magis determinatae, in umbrae reductione perseverant, sperantes se spiritus pacare posse et periculum avertere.

The witches, now more determined, persist in banishing the shadow, hoping to calm the spirits and avert danger.

Pugna cum Umbris

Sagae, corde forti, stant et manus iunctas tenent. In medio noctis, contra umbras, cantu magico valent; umbrae nunc circulum intrare non possunt.

The witches, with strong hearts, stand and hold hands. In the middle of the night, against the shadows, their magical chant is powerful; the shadows can no longer enter the circle.

"Dux spirituum venit!" Cinis timide dicit. Umbra tenebrosa, ira plena, ante eas stat.

"The leader of the spirits is coming!" Cinis says fearfully. A dark shadow, full of anger, stands before them.

Fulmina locum circum feriunt, et ventus magis augetur. Alba, non territa, invocationem antiquam recitat, suam potentiam augens.

Lightning strikes around the area, and the wind grows stronger. Alba, unafraid, recites an ancient invocation, increasing her power.

"Non intrabitis!" Bruna clamat, aquam sacram circum spargens. Subito, lumina flava circa eas creantur, spem dantia.

"You shall not enter!" Bruna shouts, sprinkling holy water around. Suddenly, yellow lights are created around them, bringing hope.

Cinis, voce forti, cantat, et voces umbrarum debilitantur. Mira res! Una umbra minor in lucem mutatur et evanescit.

Cinis, singing with a strong voice, weakens the voices of the shadows. A miraculous thing happens! One smaller shadow turns into light and vanishes.

"Videtis? Possumus vincere!" Alba exclamat, animos sagarum colligens.

"Do you see? We can win!" Alba exclaims, gathering the witches' courage.

Sed tum, umbra tenebrosa, magis furens, in circulum irruit. Confligunt, magno cum strepitu, et energia locum implet.

But then, the dark shadow, even angrier, rushes into the circle. They clash with great noise, and energy fills the place.

Subito, speculum frangitur, et vinculum inter mundos dirumpitur. Omnia silent; umbrae et sagae, momento exanimatae, stant.

Suddenly, the mirror shatters, and the bond between the worlds is broken. Everything goes silent; the shadows and the witches stand, momentarily stunned.

Tum, lumina caerulea appropinquant, pacem nuntiantia. "Quid sunt haec?" Bruna susurrat.

Then, blue lights approach, announcing peace. "What are these?" Bruna whispers.

"Num signum pacis?" Alba sperat, ad caerulea lumina spectans. Sagae, circulum stantes, miraculum spectant, corde pleno spei.

"Is this a sign of peace?" Alba hopes, watching the blue lights. The witches, standing in the circle, witness the miracle, their hearts full of hope.

Concordia

Lumina caerulea subito in formam feminae antiquae mutantur. Mulier apparet, cum voce tranquilla atque potente spectris loquens. "Pacem vobis offero," dicit.

The blue lights suddenly transform into the form of an ancient woman. She appears, speaking to the spirits with a calm yet powerful voice. "I offer you peace," she says.

Sagae, miratae et immobiles, audiunt. Non possunt movere, sed tantum spectant et audiunt. "Quis est haec?" Alba susurrat.

The witches, amazed and motionless, listen. They cannot move, but only watch and listen. "Who is she?" Alba whispers.

Spiritus, verbis mulieris auditis, placantur. Lumina eorum nunc suaviter fulgent. "Videte, pacem accipiunt," Bruna observat.

The spirits, hearing the woman's words, are calmed. Their lights now glow softly. "Look, they are accepting peace," Bruna observes.

Mulier se ad sagas vertit. "Gratias vobis ago," inquit. "Audaciam vestram laudo. Multa pericula superastis."

The woman turns to the witches. "Thank you," she says. "I praise your courage. You have overcome many dangers."

Spiritus, cum reconciliatione perfecta, ad lumina caerulea lente accedunt. Unusquisque spiritus in lumen suum ingreditur, et tranquillitas locum implet.

The spirits, now fully reconciled, slowly approach the blue lights. Each spirit enters its light, and peace fills the place.

Tum mulier se ostendit. "Ego sum custos huius loci, numen antiquum," dicit. Sagae, hoc audientes, admirantur.

Then the woman reveals herself. "I am the guardian of this place, an ancient deity," she says. The witches, hearing this, are filled with wonder.

"Venia, quaesumus, pro nostris erroribus," Cinis petit. "Nolumus ultra turbare."

"Forgive us, we ask, for our mistakes," Cinis pleads. "We do not wish to disturb any further."

Numen, clementiam ostendens, respondet: "Intelligo. Omnes errare possunt. Sed, sapientiam ex erroribus discite."

The deity, showing mercy, replies: "I understand. Everyone can make mistakes. But learn wisdom from your errors."

Sagae, gratiae plenae, promittunt se cautiores futuras esse. "Sapientiam vestram augete," numen monet.

The witches, full of gratitude, promise to be more cautious in the future. "Increase your wisdom," the deity advises.

Et sic, cum lumine claro, numen evanescit. Sagae circumspiciunt, locum pacatum et renovatum inveniunt. "Hoc custodire debemus," Alba dicit.

And so, with a bright light, the deity disappears. The witches look around and find the place peaceful and renewed. "We must protect this," Alba says.

"Videmus potentiam et periculum artis nostrae," Bruna addit.

"We see the power and danger of our craft," Bruna adds.

"Sapientiam et curam semper adhibebimus," Cinis promittit.

"We will always apply wisdom and care," Cinis promises.

Et in silva tranquilla, sub luna plena, sagae ad domos suas revertuntur, cogitationibus de nocte mirabili occupatae. Promittunt se futuros meliores custodes magiae et naturae esse. Pax et tranquillitas nunc locum et corda eorum implet, novae magiae spe inspiratae.

And in the quiet forest, under the full moon, the witches return to their homes, their minds filled with thoughts of the miraculous night. They promise to become better guardians of magic and nature. Peace and tranquility now fill the place and their hearts, inspired by the hope of new magic.

Lux et Umbra

Postquam numen, "Sapientiam vestram augete," monuit, sagae, Alba, Bruna, et Cinis, se cautiores futuras esse promittunt. Numen tum munera eis dat: herbas potentiores et lapides magicos, quae magiam earum augent.

After the deity advised, "Increase your wisdom," the witches, Alba, Bruna, and Cinis, promised to be more cautious. The deity then gave them gifts: more powerful herbs and magical stones, which enhanced their magic.

Cum lumine claro, numen evanescit. Sagae, circumspicientes, locum pacatum et renovatum inveniunt.

"Ecce, dona numinis," Alba dicit, munera in terra videns. Circulum magicum solvunt et dona colligunt, statuentes locum sacrum servare, ne malum iterum veniat.

With a bright light, the deity disappears. The witches, looking around, find the place peaceful and renewed. "Look, the gifts of the deity," Alba says, seeing the offerings on the ground. They undo the magic circle and gather the gifts, deciding to protect the sacred place so that evil will not return.

"Videmus potentiam et periculum artis nostrae," Alba gravi voce dicit, ad caelum nocturnum spectans.

"We see the power and danger of our craft," Alba says gravely, looking up at the night sky.

Bruna, manum Albae tenens, addit, "Unitae, magis sumus quam solae. Una stamus, una cadimus."

Bruna, holding Alba's hand, adds, "Together, we are stronger than alone. Together we stand, together we fall."

Cinis, ad eas conversa, serio promittit, "Sapientiam et curam semper adhibebimus. Natura et ars nostra sacra sunt."

Cinis, turning to them, solemnly promises, "We will always apply wisdom and care. Nature and our craft are sacred."

Nocte illa, luna plena et clara in caelo splendet, omnia sub lumine suo illuminans. Sonus silvae tranquillus redit, et animalia nocturna, sicut noctuae et lupi, iterum audiri possunt.

That night, the full and bright moon shines in the sky, illuminating everything with its light. The peaceful sound of the forest returns, and nocturnal animals, like owls and wolves, can be heard again.

Sagae leniter ad suas domos revertuntur, mente plenae cogitationibus de nocte mirabili. Promittunt se meliores custodes magiae et naturae futuras esse, semper memores verborum numinis et potentiae artis suae.

The witches gently return to their homes, their minds full of thoughts about the miraculous night. They promise to be better guardians of magic and nature, always remembering the deity's words and the power of their craft.

Pax profunda locum et corda eorum implet. In lumine lunae et silentio noctis, spes nova de futura magia in eis crescit, sperantes se mundum meliorem facturas.

A deep peace fills the place and their hearts. In the moonlight and the silence of the night, a new hope for future magic grows within them, as they hope to make the world better.

Villa Spectris Lusor

In Villa Mysteriis Plena

Nocte una in villa divitis Romani, cui nomen Gaius est, res mirae coeperunt. Gaius cum familia sua cenabat, cum subito servus Lupus sonos insolitos ex horto audire se dixit.

One night in the villa of a wealthy Roman named Gaius, strange things began to happen. Gaius was dining with his family when suddenly the servant Lupus said he heard unusual sounds from the garden.

"Domine, sonos mirabiles in horto audivi!" Lupus exclamat.

"Master, I heard strange sounds in the garden!" Lupus exclaimed.

Gaius, non serio accipiens, ridet et respondet, "Fortassis ventris tui sonus est, non spectri!"

Gaius, not taking it seriously, laughed and replied, "Perhaps it's the sound of your stomach, not a ghost!"

Sed media nocte, Gaius ipse sonum audivit et ex lecto exsiluit. Tota familia excitata est; "Spectrum per villam nostram vagatur!" Gaius exclamavit.

But in the middle of the night, Gaius himself heard the sound and jumped out of bed. The whole family was awakened; "A ghost is wandering through our villa!" Gaius exclaimed.

Servi, qui magis magisque timebant, "Minime, domine, minime!" negabant. Sed Gaius, vir audax, "Inquiramus!" dixit.

The servants, growing more and more frightened, denied it, saying, "No, master, no!" But Gaius, being a brave man, said, "Let's investigate!"

Cum lintea ut scuta gerentes et candelas ut gladios tenentes, ad hortum caute processerunt. Ventus repente valvas clauserat. "Factum spectri!" Gaius exclamavit.

Holding sheets as shields and candles as swords, they cautiously proceeded to the garden. The wind suddenly slammed the doors. "A ghost's doing!" Gaius exclaimed.

Adhuc in horto, statua Veneris quasi moveri coepisse videbatur. "Ecce! Venus ipsa nos salutat!" Lupus, territus, susurravit.

Still in the garden, the statue of Venus seemed to begin moving. "Look! Venus herself greets us!" Lupus whispered in fear.

Sed subito, lumen ex una fenestrarum villae fulsit. "Ecce lumen spectri!" clamat omnis familia, in villam regressura.

But suddenly, light flashed from one of the villa's windows. "Behold the light of the ghost!" the whole family shouted, about to return inside.

Sed cum intraverunt, omnia tranquilla erant; nullum signum spectri vel luminis. "Ludibrium spectri hoc est," Gaius serio dixit. "Cras diligentius inquiramus quid hoc sit!"

But when they entered, everything was calm; there was no sign of the ghost or the light. "This is the prank of a ghost," Gaius said seriously. "Tomorrow, let's investigate more thoroughly what this is!"

Et sic, initium inquisitionis de mysterio villae fecerunt, parati investigare quid spectri desideraret et cur eos in ludos trahebat.

And so, they began the investigation of the villa's mystery, ready to explore what the ghost wanted and why it was drawing them into its games.

Vestigia Spectri

Prima luce, Gaius familiaque eius consilium novum capiunt: spectrum quaerere decernunt.

At first light, Gaius and his family make a new decision: they decide to search for the ghost.

"In bibliotheca incipiemus," Gaius dicit, "Ibi sunt libri de spectris."

"We will begin in the library," Gaius says, "There are books about ghosts there."

Dum per libros scrutantur, subito folium a vento movetur, quasi ducatur. "Sequimini!" Gaius iubet, et omnes folium sequuntur, quod eos ad cellam mysteriosam ducit.

While they search through the books, suddenly a page is moved by the wind, as if it's being guided. "Follow it!" Gaius commands, and they all follow the page, which leads them to a mysterious room.

In cella, vinum ex amphora sine ullius manus auxilio effunditur. "Spectro bibendum videtur!" Lupus, oculis magnis, exclamat.

In the room, wine pours from an amphora without the help of any hand. "The ghost seems to want a drink!" Lupus exclaims, wide-eyed.

Sub rete aranearum tabulam scriptoriam antiquam pulvere tectam inveniunt. "Spectro communicemus!" Gaius suadet.

Under a spider's web, they find an ancient writing tablet covered in dust. "Let's communicate with the ghost!" Gaius suggests.

Ad tabulam sedentes, spiritus per manum ducit litteras: N-O-N S-O-L-I. "Non soli sumus," Lupus tremens interpretatur.

Sitting at the tablet, the spirit guides their hand to write the letters: N-O-N S-O-L-I. "We are not alone," Lupus tremblingly interprets.

Tum, per silentium, risus infantis per auras fertur, quod omnibus terrorem incutit, nam infans nullus in villa est. Et statua canis, custos domus, quasi ad portam spectare videtur.

Then, through the silence, a baby's laughter is carried through the air, filling everyone with terror, for there is no baby in the villa. And the statue of the dog, the guardian of the house, seems to be looking toward the door.

"Aliquid foris est," Gaius susurrat, et omnes celeriter ad fenestram currunt.

"Something is outside," Gaius whispers, and they all quickly run to the window.

Foris, praeter nebulam densam nihil vident, quae subito ante eos apparet. Et ex nebula, figura obscura et vaga, sed forma non clara, quasi emergit.

Outside, they see nothing but a dense fog, which suddenly appears before them. And from the fog, a dark and vague figure, but not clearly formed, seems to emerge.

Revertentes ad ianuam, mirantur eam clausam esse. "Ubi clavis est?" Lupus interrogat, sed nemo respondet.

Returning to the door, they are surprised to find it closed. "Where is the key?" Lupus asks, but no one answers.

Gaius, ponderans, "Forte placandum est spectrum," dicit. "Donum ei quaeramus."

Gaius, pondering, says, "Perhaps the ghost needs to be appeased. Let's find it a gift."

Omnes ad consilium Gaii assentiunt, statuentes donum in horto ponere, ut benignum spectri animum concilient. "Sed quid spectris placet?" interrogant, ad novam inquisitionem parati.

Everyone agrees with Gaius' plan, deciding to place a gift in the garden to win the ghost's favor. "But what do ghosts like?" they ask, ready for a new investigation.

Munus Spectro

Nocte illa, sub lumine stellarum, Gaius et familia eius in hortum procedunt, donum spectro parati offerre.

That night, under the starlight, Gaius and his family proceed to the garden, ready to offer a gift to the ghost.

"Quid amant spectra?" Lupus, caput inclinans, rogat.

"What do ghosts love?" Lupus asks, tilting his head.

Gaius, considerans, respondet, "Pacem amant. Florem pacis in horto collocemus."

Gaius, thinking, responds, "They love peace. Let us place a flower of peace in the garden."

Cum floribus eleganter in terra dispositis, subito terra tremit. "Spectro donum placet!" Gaius, laetus, exclamat.

As the flowers are elegantly placed in the ground, the earth suddenly trembles. "The ghost likes the gift!" Gaius exclaims happily.

Tremore cessante, tranquillitas redit. Sed, inter silentium, vocem feminam audire videntur. "Auxilium meum invenire debetis," leniter susurrat.

As the trembling ceases, tranquility returns. But in the silence, they seem to hear a woman's voice. "You must find my help," she gently whispers.

Circumspiciunt, quaerentes unde vox veniat, sed soli sunt. "Femina est quae nos adiuvare vult," Gaius, voce gravi, affirmat.

They look around, searching for the source of the voice, but they are alone. "It is a woman who wants to help us," Gaius affirms in a serious tone.

"Quomodo te adiuvare possumus?" Gaius in tenebras clamat.

"How can we help you?" Gaius shouts into the darkness.

Vox, quasi vento portata, respondet, "Sub arbusto rosae clavem quaerite."

The voice, carried by the wind, responds, "Search under the rose bush for the key."

Ad arbustum properant et terram fodiunt, quaerentes quid ibi celatur. Brevi tempore, inveniunt clavem antiquam, a lunae lumine illuminatam.

They hurry to the rose bush and dig into the ground, searching for what is hidden there. In a short time, they find an ancient key, illuminated by the moonlight.

Lupus, clavem inspiciens, "Quid hoc aperit?" interrogat.

Lupus, examining the key, asks, "What does this open?"

"Arcanum in villa est quod hac clavi aperiemus," Gaius, mysterio plenus, dicit. "Cras explorabimus quid celatur."

"There is a secret in the villa that we will open with this key," Gaius, full of mystery, says. "Tomorrow, we will explore what is hidden."

Omnes, pleni curiositate et timore mixto, ad domum revertuntur, cogitantes de arcano quod cras revelabunt. "Spectri aenigma speramus solvere," Gaius dicit, dum in silentium noctis ambulant.

All, filled with a mixture of curiosity and fear, return to the house, thinking about the secret they will reveal tomorrow. "We hope to solve the ghost's riddle," Gaius says, as they walk in the silence of the night.

Arcanum Revelatum

Cum primum lux diei villam Gaii illuminat, familia congregatur ad clavem inspiciendam, quam nocte priore invenerunt.

As the first light of day illuminates Gaius' villa, the family gathers to inspect the key they found the night before.

Gaius, clavem in manu tenens, reminiscitur de ianua secreta in villa. "Forsitan ad cryptam ducit!" Lupus, oculis magnis, exclamat.

Gaius, holding the key in his hand, recalls the secret door in the villa. "Perhaps it leads to the crypt!" Lupus exclaims, eyes wide.

Ianuam in fundo villae reperiunt, clavemque tentant. Cum clavis ianuam aperit, scalae quae ad tenebrosas profunditates descendunt se ostendunt.

They find the door at the bottom of the villa and try the key. When the key opens the door, stairs leading down into dark depths reveal themselves.

"Descendamus," Gaius fortiter dicit, et omnes lumina accendunt descendereque incipiunt.

"Let's descend," Gaius says firmly, and they all light their torches and begin to descend.

In fundo, cryptam inveniunt, in qua sarcophagus apertus eos exspectat. "Quis hic dormit?" Gaius susurrans interrogat, ad sarcophagum accedens.

At the bottom, they find a crypt where an open sarcophagus awaits them. "Who sleeps here?" Gaius whispers, approaching the sarcophagus.

Lupus, cum audacia falsa, sarcophagum aperit. Intra, ossa antiqua reperiuntur. Inter ossa, tabula parva est cum inscriptione: "Vindictam quaero."

Lupus, with false bravery, opens the sarcophagus. Inside, ancient bones are found. Among the bones, there is a small tablet with the inscription: "I seek vengeance."

"Spectro iniustitia accidit," Gaius, frontem corrugans, cogitat.

"The ghost suffered an injustice," Gaius thinks, furrowing his brow.

Tum, vocem audiunt: "Vindictam meam adiuvate."

Then they hear a voice: "Help me in my vengeance."

"Quis te iniuria affecit?" Gaius, in tenebris clamans, interrogat.

"Who wronged you?" Gaius shouts into the darkness.

"Familia mea... proditione," tristis vox respondet.

"My family... by betrayal," the sorrowful voice replies.

"Te iustitia donabo," Gaius, solemniter promittit.

"I will give you justice," Gaius solemnly promises.

"Gratias tibi ago," vox dicit, et subito crypta lumine fulget, tamquam sol ipse intus luceret.

"Thank you," the voice says, and suddenly the crypt glows with light, as if the sun itself were shining inside.

Omnes, lumine circumdati, stant in silentio, promissionem Gaii considerantes. "Inveniemus veritatem," Gaius dicit, "et pacem spectri restituemus."

All, surrounded by the light, stand in silence, contemplating Gaius' promise. "We will find the truth," Gaius says, "and we will restore the ghost's peace."

Hac promissione facta, familia ascendit ad lucem diei, parata ad investigandum et ad spectri desiderium complendum.

With this promise made, the family ascends into the daylight, ready to investigate and fulfill the ghost's desire.

In Iustitiam

Gaius et familia eius, post revelationem in crypta, decernunt spectri causam investigare. Historiam villae perquirunt, sperantes iustitiam spectro afferre posse.

Gaius and his family, after the revelation in the crypt, decide to investigate the cause of the ghost. They search through the villa's history, hoping to bring justice to the spirit.

In bibliotheca villae, cum multos libros et tabulas veteres scrutantur, veritatem inveniunt. "Ecce!" Lupus exclamat, tabulam demonstrans. "Antiquus dominus villae sororem suam proditione accusavit!"

In the villa's library, as they sift through many books and old records, they discover the truth. "Look!" Lupus exclaims, pointing to a record. "The villa's former master accused his sister of betrayal!"

Gaius, tabulam inspectans, "Iustitiam spectri restituemus," certo animo dicit.

Gaius, inspecting the record, says with determination, "We will restore the ghost's justice."

Consilium capiunt ut caeremoniam in horto faciant, circulum magicum parantes ut iustitiam vocent. "Hoc spectri animam pacabit," Gaius sperat.

They plan to perform a ceremony in the garden, preparing a magic circle to call for justice. "This will bring peace to the ghost's soul," Gaius hopes.

Caeremoniam incipiunt, et subito ventus fortis surgit, circulum magicum movens. E tenebris, vox spectri auditur: "Soror mea, vindictam meam completa!"

They begin the ceremony, and suddenly a strong wind rises, shaking the magic circle. From the darkness, the ghost's voice is heard: "My sister, complete my vengeance!"

Tum, ante eos, figura feminina, claritate plena, apparet. "Adiuvare te venimus," Gaius, manum extendens, dicit. "Pacem tuam quaere."

Then, before them, a female figure full of light appears. "We have come to help you," Gaius says, extending his hand. "Seek your peace."

Spectro, ad eos converso, oculi eius gratiam profundam ostendunt. "Familia mea iniuriam mihi fecit," triste narrat. "Sed vos mihi pacem dedistis."

The ghost, turning toward them, shows deep gratitude in her eyes. "My family wronged me," she sadly recounts. "But you have given me peace."

"Iustitia facta est," alia vox, magis masculina, adiungit, et figura viri paenitentis apparet. "Soror, ignosce mihi," vir spectri rogat.

"Justice has been done," another, more masculine voice adds, and a figure of a repentant man appears. "Sister, forgive me," the ghostly man pleads.

Mulier spectri, diu considerans, tandem respondet: "Ignosco tibi." Et in momento, ambo figurae in lucem pulchram solvuntur, quasi liberatae.

The female ghost, after long consideration, finally responds: "I forgive you." And in that moment, both figures dissolve into a beautiful light, as if they have been freed.

Gaius, circumspiciens ad familiam suam, "Pacem tandem invenerunt," dicit, "Eorum spiritus nunc liberi sunt."

Gaius, looking around at his family, says, "They have finally found peace. Their spirits are now free."

Familia, spectaculo commota, in silentio stant, gratias agentes quod adiuvare potuerunt. "Per iustitiam et concordiam verus pacis sensus invenitur," Gaius, stellas in caelo nocturno spectans, affirmat.

The family, moved by the spectacle, stands in silence, grateful that they were able to help. "Through justice and harmony, the true sense of peace is found," Gaius affirms, gazing at the stars in the night sky.

Post Iustitiam

Postquam iustitia spectris data est, villa nova tranquillitate fruitur.

After justice was given to the spirits, the villa enjoys a new tranquility.

"Spectra amica beneficia nobis dederunt," Gaius, per hortum ambulans, observat. Circumstant flores pulcherrimi, quasi nocte ipsa florescerent.

"The friendly spirits have bestowed blessings upon us," Gaius observes, walking through the garden. Beautiful flowers surround them, as if they bloomed during the night itself.

Servi, qui olim timore palluerant, nunc cum gaudio inter se laborant. "Videsne? Nunc etiam aurae laetiores sunt," Alba, floribus odoratis in manibus, adiungit.

The servants, who once paled with fear, now work together with joy. "Do you see? Even the air feels lighter now," Alba adds, holding fragrant flowers in her hands.

Familia saepe in sermone meminit amicorum spectralium, eorum gratitudinem exprimens. "Semper in corde nostro et in villa nostra manebunt," Gaius solemniter promittit.

The family often speaks of their spectral friends, expressing their gratitude. "They will always remain in our hearts and in our villa," Gaius solemnly promises.

Noctu, in horto, lucem suavem vident, quasi signum pacis a spectralibus amicis missum. Gaius, in honorem eorum, statuam ponit, sempiternam gratitudinem demonstrans.

At night, they see a soft light in the garden, as if a sign of peace from their spectral friends. Gaius places a statue in their honor, showing eternal gratitude.

Curiosi de miraculo audientes, ad villam veniunt, historiam spectri et reconciliationis audire cupientes. Villa cito famosa efficitur, quasi pharus pacis et historiae antiquae.

Curious people, hearing of the miracle, come to the villa, eager to hear the story of the ghost and reconciliation. The villa quickly becomes famous, like a beacon of peace and ancient history.

"Exemplum nobis praebent," Gaius advenis narrat, "de magnitudine iustitiae et potestate reconciliationis."

"They provide us with an example," Gaius tells the visitors, "of the greatness of justice and the power of reconciliation."

Nunc, familia alios adiuvare nititur, inspirationem a spectralibus amicis trahens. "In difficiliis, meminisse debemus amorem et iustitiam esse claves," Gaius in festis loquitur, historiae spectrorum particeps.

Now, the family strives to help others, drawing inspiration from their spectral friends. "In difficult times, we must remember that love and justice are the keys," Gaius says during festivals, sharing the story of the ghosts.

Visitatores, villa relicta, pacem profundam sentiunt, miraculum quod spectra creaverunt admirantes. "Haec

*historia non solum de spectralibus est, sed etiam de nobis,"
quidam susurrat.*

Visitors, upon leaving the villa, feel a deep peace, marveling
at the miracle the ghosts created. "This story is not only about
the spirits, but also about us," someone whispers.

*Gaius, in vita nova, se dedicat servandi et adiuvandi alios,
a spectralibus amicis docetur. "Per eos, viam meliorem
invenimus," dicit, ad caelum nocturnum spectans, gratias
agens pro nova vita et missione.*

Gaius, in his new life, dedicates himself to helping and
serving others, taught by his spectral friends. "Through them,
we have found a better path," he says, gazing at the night sky,
giving thanks for his new life and mission.

Pax Aeterna

*Anniversario illius ceremoniae magicae, Gaius cum familia
sua iterum in hortum conveniunt, locum ubi omnia coeperunt.*

On the anniversary of that magical ceremony, Gaius and his
family gather again in the garden, the place where it all began.

*"Honoremus hodie amicos nostros spectri," Gaius, flores et
vinum in ara parans, dicit. "Gratias eis agamus pro pace nobis
data."*

"Let us honor our spectral friends today," says Gaius,
preparing flowers and wine on the altar. "Let us thank them for
the peace they have given us."

*Dum silentio flores et vinum offerunt, terra subito levi
tremore movetur, quasi spectri eorum praesentiam salutent.
"Nos sentiunt," Lupus, miratus, susurrat.*

As they offer flowers and wine in silence, the ground
suddenly trembles slightly, as if the spirits are greeting their
presence. "They can feel us," Lupus whispers in awe.

*Tunc, vox suavis, quasi vento portata, ad eos pervenit:
"Gratias vobis." Vox calida et consolans est.*

Then, a gentle voice, carried on the wind, reaches them: "Thank you." The voice is warm and comforting.

Subito, caelum nocturnum stellis incredibiliter illuminatur, tamquam caelestis chorea initur. "Videte caelum!" Lupus, admirans, clamat.

Suddenly, the night sky is illuminated with incredible stars, as if a celestial dance begins. "Look at the sky!" Lupus exclaims in wonder.

Et inter stellas, figurae spectralium amicorum brevi fulgore apparent, quasi pacem et amorem ad terram mittentes. "Pacem vobiscum," omnes, manibus iunctis, dicunt.

And among the stars, the figures of their spectral friends appear briefly in a radiant glow, as if sending peace and love to the earth. "Peace be with you," they all say, holding hands.

Circumstantes calidum et amabilem sensum sentiunt, tamquam amplexu amicorum spectralium involvantur. "Nos semper custodient," Alba, voce molli, affirmat.

Those gathered feel a warm and loving sensation, as if embraced by their spectral friends. "They will always watch over us," Alba affirms softly.

Illius noctis, dulcia somnia de amicis spectralibus habent, quasi ad eos visendi venissent. Somnia plena amoris et pacis sunt.

That night, they have sweet dreams of their spectral friends, as if the spirits came to visit them. The dreams are full of love and peace.

Cum aurora advenit, omnes renovati surgunt, cordibus plenis gratitudinis pro vita mutata et amicitiis aeternis. "Vita nostra per eos melior facta est," Gaius, ad solis ortum, meditatur.

When dawn arrives, they all rise renewed, their hearts filled with gratitude for their transformed lives and eternal friendships. "Our lives have been made better by them," Gaius reflects as the sun rises.

Ad statuam amicorum spectralium, Gaius promittit: "Memoria vestra et amor dux nobis erit in omnibus actis nostris."

At the statue of their spectral friends, Gaius promises: "Your memory and love will guide us in all our actions."

Villa, quae olim timore et mysterio plena erat, nunc exemplar est pacis et concordiae, lucem in tenebris praebens. "Haec est vera hereditas nostra," Gaius familiae narrat.

The villa, which was once full of fear and mystery, is now a symbol of peace and harmony, offering light in the darkness. "This is our true heritage," Gaius tells his family.

Gaius, in contemplatione profunda, concludit: "Per amicitiam et iustitiam, veram pacem invenimus. Spectra nos docuerunt quomodo vivere debemus—in amore, iustitia, et pace."

In deep contemplation, Gaius concludes: "Through friendship and justice, we have found true peace. The spirits taught us how we should live—in love, justice, and peace."

Et sic, villa, quae olim locus terroris erat, nunc est pharus pacis et amoris, testimonium quod per amicitiam et iustitiam, etiam in profundis tenebris, lux et pax aeterna inveniri possunt.

And so, the villa, which was once a place of terror, is now a beacon of peace and love, a testament that through friendship and justice, even in the deepest darkness, eternal light and peace can be found.

Nox ad Murum Hadriani

Adventus ad Murum

Turistae ad Murum Hadriani veniunt, antiquam munitionem Romanorum. Dies brevis est et cito obscuratur, quia November est.

The tourists arrive at Hadrian's Wall, the ancient Roman fortification. The day is short and quickly darkens, because it is November.

"Laeti sumus hodie murum videre," dicit unus turista.

"We are happy to see the wall today," says one tourist.

"Sed parum scimus de historia huius loci," alter respondet.

"But we know little about the history of this place," another responds.

Dux, qui eos ducit, inquit, "Multas fabulas habeo de Romanis et Pictis vobis narrare."

The guide, leading them, says, "I have many stories to tell you about the Romans and the Picts."

Cum ambulant, nubes in caelo congregantur et ventus frigidus spirat.

As they walk, clouds gather in the sky, and a cold wind blows.

"Ad locum castrorum Romanorum nunc vos duco," dux annuntiat.

"Now I lead you to the site of the Roman fort," the guide announces.

Sed subito, nebula densa circum eos apparet, et omnes perterriti sunt.

But suddenly, a dense fog appears around them, and everyone is frightened.

"Quid est hoc?" turista exclamat. "Sonitus armorum audire possumus!"

"What is this?" exclaims a tourist. "We can hear the sound of weapons!"

Dux, tranquillus, respondet, "Saepius hic mira accidunt. Murus Hadriani plenus est mysteriis."

The guide, calm, replies, "Strange things often happen here. Hadrian's Wall is full of mysteries."

Cum obscuritas crescit, turistae prope murum manent, sonitus belli circum eos audientes.

As the darkness grows, the tourists remain near the wall, hearing the sounds of battle around them.

Formae incertae in nebula moveri incipiunt.

Uncertain shapes begin to move in the fog.

Dux monet, "Statis tranquilli. Hic, historia ad vitam venit."

The guide warns, "Stay calm. Here, history comes to life."

Turistae nunc murmura et clamores audire incipiunt, corde trementes.

The tourists now begin to hear murmurs and shouts, their hearts trembling.

Et subito, ex nebula, spectri Pictorum apparent, ad murum cum furore currunt.

And suddenly, out of the fog, the ghosts of the Picts appear, running fiercely toward the wall.

"Videte! Spectra!" turista clamat.

"Look! Ghosts!" a tourist shouts.

"Suntne illi... veri?" alter quaerit, oculis magnis.

"Are they... real?" another asks, eyes wide.

Dux, manum elevans, "Spectaculum est unicum," dicit. "Hi sunt animae antiquae qui adhuc suas pugnas pugnant."

The guide, raising his hand, says, "This is a unique spectacle. These are ancient souls who still fight their battles."

Turistae, medio terrore et admiratione, spectant. Nox ad Murum Hadriani modo coepit, et iam mirabilia promittit.

The tourists, caught between terror and awe, watch. The night at Hadrian's Wall has just begun, and it already promises wonders.

Noctis Proelium

Turistae, timore pleni, incipiunt retrocedere.

The tourists, full of fear, begin to retreat.

"Dux, nonne hoc periculum magnum est?" unus ex eis trepidat.

"Guide, isn't this a great danger?" one of them trembles.

Dux, manu ad pacem invitans, "Manete, quaeso. Historiae partem vivimus," eos hortatur.

The guide, raising his hand in a calming gesture, urges them, "Stay, please. We are living part of history."

In campo ante eos, spectra Pictorum armis priscis instructa, magnis clamoribus apparuerunt.

In the field before them, the ghosts of the Picts, armed with ancient weapons, appear with loud shouts.

Subito, caelum tonitruis magnis et fulminibus impletur.

Suddenly, the sky fills with great thunder and lightning.

"Ecce! Romani etiam adveniunt!" alter turista exclamat, cum spectra legionariorum ex altera parte muri appareant.

"Look! The Romans are coming too!" another tourist exclaims, as the ghosts of legionaries appear on the other side of the wall.

Legiones spectrales se ad pugnam ordinant, Pictis obviam iturae.

The spectral legions arrange themselves for battle, preparing to meet the Picts.

"Media in acie spectrorum nos invenimus," turista susurrat, miratus.

"We find ourselves in the middle of a ghostly battle," a tourist whispers in amazement.

Picti spectri ad murum cum clamoribus ferocibus procedunt.

The ghostly Picts advance toward the wall with ferocious cries.

Romani, militari disciplina utentes, murum strenue defendunt.

The Romans, using military discipline, defend the wall vigorously.

"Num hoc verum est?" turista sub murmure quaerit.

"Is this real?" the tourist murmurs under his breath.

Dux, circumstantibus explicans, "Hae animae priscas luctas suas hic peragunt."

The guide explains to those around, "These souls are reenacting their ancient struggles here."

Saxa et tela spectralia mirabiliter per aera volitant, turistas tamen non attingunt.

Stones and ghostly weapons miraculously fly through the air, yet do not touch the tourists.

Clamor et tumultus crescunt, quasi in medio realis praelii sint.

The noise and tumult grow, as if they were in the middle of a real battle.

Frigus subitum omnes invadit, ad ossa usque penetrans.

A sudden chill invades everyone, penetrating to their bones.

Cum clamor ad climax ascendit, repente omnia in silentium cadunt.

As the noise reaches its peak, suddenly everything falls silent.

Turistae et dux in expectando silentio manent, futurum quid paraturum.

The tourists and the guide remain in expectant silence, waiting for what will come next.

In Muro Inter Spectra

Turistae circumspiciunt, admirantes quod proelium spectrale subito pausat.

The tourists look around, marveling at how the ghostly battle suddenly halts.

Nebula circum eos densior fit, paene nihil videntes. Exercitus spectrorum ad invicem respiciunt, immobiles.

The fog around them grows denser, making it hard to see anything. The armies of specters gaze at each other, motionless.

Dux susurrat, "In momento magico sumus. Haec est historia viva."

The guide whispers, "We are in a magical moment. This is living history."

Turistae sentiunt quasi tempus se aliter movere, historiae testes facti.

The tourists feel as if time moves differently, having become witnesses to history.

Romani, in ordine stricto, silentium tenent, murum defendentes.

The Romans, in strict formation, remain silent, defending the wall.

Spectra Pictorum, oculis plenis ferociae, expectant.

The ghostly Picts, their eyes filled with ferocity, stand waiting.

"Est frigidus," dicit turista, "sed haec mira sunt, non timenda."

"It's cold," says a tourist, "but these sights are incredible, not frightening."

Dux eos cautius per nebulam ducit, ad acies spectrorum propius.

The guide carefully leads them through the fog, closer to the lines of specters.

Turistae spectant et audiunt, sed nil tangunt. "Historiam vivam videtis," dux iterum dicit.

The tourists watch and listen, but touch nothing. "You are seeing living history," the guide says again.

Picti, clamores bellicos renovantes, ad pugnam parati stant.

The Picts, renewing their war cries, stand ready for battle.

Romani scuta levant et gladios stringunt, parati ad defendendum.

The Romans raise their shields and draw their swords, ready to defend.

Turistae in medio haerent, quasi somnium vivant, praelium expectantes.

The tourists stand frozen in the middle, as if living a dream, awaiting the battle.

Et subito, cum magno tumultu, praelium spectrale iterum incipit.

And suddenly, with great commotion, the ghostly battle begins again.

Culmen Proelii

Turistae stant in admiratione, spectantes Romanos spectros qui acriter pugnant.

The tourists stand in awe, watching the Roman ghosts who fight fiercely.

Picti, scalis ad murum appositis, conantur Romanos repellere.

The Picts, with ladders placed against the wall, try to drive back the Romans.

Dux turistis susurrat, "Ultimum proelium testes estis."

The guide whispers to the tourists, "You are witnessing the final battle."

Etsi ventus et sonitus proelii circumsonant, turistae securi sunt, sine ulla noxia.

Though wind and the sounds of battle surround them, the tourists are safe, without any harm.

Caelum clamoribus spectrorum et sonitu armorum impletur, graven metum efficiens.

The sky is filled with the cries of the ghosts and the clash of weapons, creating a heavy sense of dread.

"Hic est locus," dux explicat, "ubi historia et fabula se iungunt."

"This is the place," the guide explains, "where history and legend come together."

Turistae animadvertunt Pictos spectros muro propius venientes, dum Romani eos excipiunt.

The tourists notice the ghostly Picts drawing closer to the wall, while the Romans intercept them.

Subito, nebula colorem rubrum assumit, quasi sanguinem antiquum memoret.

Suddenly, the fog takes on a red hue, as if recalling ancient bloodshed.

Frigus intensum est, sed turistae, pulsationibus suis auditis, proelium spectant.

The cold is intense, but the tourists, hearing their own heartbeats, watch the battle.

In campo aperto, spectra legionariorum cum Pictis spectris fervide confligunt.

In the open field, the ghostly legions clash fiercely with the ghostly Picts.

Pugna adeo intensa est, ut turistae terram tremere sub pedibus sentire videantur.

The fight is so intense that the tourists seem to feel the ground trembling beneath their feet.

"Spectra pro locis suis et honoribus dimicant," dux narrat, spectaculum monstrans.

"The ghosts are fighting for their land and honor," the guide explains, showing the scene.

Turistae spectrorum audaciam et fortitudinem admirantur, quasi in historiae paginis vivant.

The tourists admire the bravery and strength of the ghosts, as if they are living within the pages of history.

Tum, subito, maior figura spectralis in medio proelii apparet, qui dux esse videtur.

Then, suddenly, a larger ghostly figure appears in the middle of the battle, who seems to be the leader.

Hic dux spectralis manum elevat, et, mirum dictu, omnia spectra ad silentium veniunt.

This ghostly leader raises his hand, and, astonishingly, all the ghosts fall silent.

Pax Aeterna

Turistae et dux in silentio spectant, dum spectra immobilia stant.

The tourists and the guide watch in silence as the ghosts stand motionless.

Dux spectralis, magna voce, "Pacem vobis do," dicit.

The ghostly leader, in a loud voice, says, "I give you peace."

Turistae, etsi in nebula frigida sunt, calorem mirum sentiunt.

The tourists, though in the cold mist, feel a strange warmth.

Spectra Romanorum et Pictorum se respiciunt, manibus pacem signantes.

The ghosts of the Romans and the Picts look at each other, signaling peace with their hands.

Dux ad turistas vertit, "In tenebris etiam, pax nasci potest."

The leader turns to the tourists and says, "Even in darkness, peace can be born."

Turistae vident spectra, quae olim inimica erant, nunc se amplectentia.

The tourists see the ghosts, once enemies, now embracing each other.

Nebula paulatim evanescit, et stellae in caelo clarius lucent.

The mist gradually fades, and the stars shine brighter in the sky.

"Hoc fuit proelium ultimum. Nunc animae requiem inveniunt," dux narrat.

"This was the final battle. Now the souls find rest," the guide explains.

Spectra sensim desinunt, velut in aetherem solvuntur.

The ghosts slowly fade away, as if dissolving into the ether.

Turistae pacem profundam sentiunt, velut momenti historici testes.

The tourists feel a deep peace, as if they are witnesses to a historic moment.

Ad murum dux eos ducit, ubi nunc regnat silentium profundum.

The guide leads them to the wall, where a profound silence now reigns.

Turistae, contemplantes quae acciderunt, in silentio stant.

The tourists, contemplating what has happened, stand in silence.

Antequam abeunt, flores ad murum ponunt, parvam caerimoniam pacis facientes.

Before they leave, they place flowers at the wall, performing a small ceremony of peace.

Cum prima luce solis, turistae domum revertuntur, corde pleni mysteriis quae viderunt.

With the first light of the sun, the tourists return home, their hearts filled with the mysteries they have witnessed.

Dux ultimo dicit, "Haec nox in memoria vestra semper manebit, monstrans pacem et historiam simul ire."

The guide says at last, "This night will forever remain in your memory, showing that peace and history walk together."

Spectrum et Servus

Intrigae Introductio

Londinii, legati palatium magnificum est. Gaius, servus callidus, semper dominum suum, legatum, decipere conatur.

In London, the ambassador's palace is magnificent. Gaius, a clever servant, always tries to deceive his master, the ambassador.

Intra moenia palatii, larva ludens, quam Spectrum vocamus, habitat. Legatus, vir severus, de his mysteriis palatii nihil scit.

Within the walls of the palace, a playful ghost, which we call Spectrum, resides. The ambassador, a strict man, knows nothing of the palace's mysteries.

Una nocte, Gaius vinum legati furtim capit. Dum in angulo obscuro vinum bibit, subito Spectrum primum conspicit.

One night, Gaius secretly steals the ambassador's wine. While drinking in a dark corner, he suddenly sees Spectrum for the first time.

Spectrum, subridens, Gaium observat. "Salve, Gaie!" Spectrum inquit. "Ludere vis?"

Spectrum, smiling, watches Gaius. "Hello, Gaius!" Spectrum says. "Do you want to play?"

Gaius, primo territus, mox curiosus fit. "Quis es? Et quid ludere vis?" rogat.

Gaius, initially frightened, soon becomes curious. "Who are you? And what game do you want to play?" he asks.

Spectrum respondet: "Noli timere, Gaie. Non tibi nocebo. Ludum simplicem ludere volo."

Spectrum replies: "Do not be afraid, Gaius. I won't harm you. I just want to play a simple game."

Gaius, animo paulum recreatus, consensit. "Bene," inquit, "sed meminisse debeo te superare."

Gaius, somewhat reassured, agrees. "Alright," he says, "but remember, I have to beat you."

Spectrum, ad ludum paratum, dolum primum suum meditatur. "Videbimus," Spectrum cum risu inquit. "Paratusne es ad ludum nostrum?"

Spectrum, ready for the game, prepares his first trick. "We shall see," Spectrum says with a grin. "Are you ready for our game?"

Et ita, sub lumine lunae, ludus inter Gaium servum et Spectrum, larvam ludicram, incipit. Inter vasa vinaria et umbras palatii, mysterium et risus coalescunt, sicut in fabulis Plauti legimus.

And so, under the light of the moon, the game between Gaius the servant and Spectrum, the playful ghost, begins. Among the wine barrels and shadows of the palace, mystery and laughter come together, as we read in the comedies of Plautus.

Gaius, licet cautus, a Spectro ad ludum provocatur. Spectrum, per noctem ducens, Gaium in varias partes palatii invitat, ubi primum dolum suum exsequitur.

Gaius, though cautious, is challenged by Spectrum to play. Leading him through the night, Spectrum invites Gaius into various parts of the palace, where he executes his first trick.

"Videamus," Spectrum susurrat, "si me in hoc palatio invenire potes. Si potes, vinum tibi praemium erit."

"Let's see," Spectrum whispers, "if you can find me in this palace. If you do, the wine will be your reward."

Provocatione accepta, Gaius per tenebrosas aulas palatii quaerere coepit. Ita nocturna coniunctio, plena risu et terrore, exordium capit.

With the challenge accepted, Gaius begins to search through the dark halls of the palace. Thus, a nocturnal encounter, full of laughter and terror, begins.

Alea Vinaria

In profundis palatii legati, cella vinaria secreta celatur. Hic conveniunt Spectrum, spiritus ludicrus, et Gaius, servus callidus et astutus.

In the depths of the ambassador's palace, a secret wine cellar is hidden. Here meet Spectrum, the playful spirit, and Gaius, the clever and cunning servant.

"Spectrum," Gaius inquit, "ubi est illud vinum quod promisisti?"

"Spectrum," Gaius says, "where is that wine you promised?"

Spectrum, risu leni, respondet, "Invenire opus est tibi. Si potes, vinum optimum tibi dabo."

Spectrum, with a soft laugh, replies, "You must find it. If you can, I will give you the finest wine."

Gaius, lucernam firmans, per obscura palatii itinera incedit. Spectrum, arte magica utitur, creans sonos terribiles et imagines quae terrorem incutiant. Gaius, quamquam perterritus, non cessat.

Gaius, securing his lantern, walks through the dark corridors of the palace. Spectrum uses magic, creating terrifying sounds and images meant to frighten. Gaius, though scared, does not stop.

Repente, Spectrum coram Gaium apparet, risu pleno. "Invenisti me, Gaie! Accipe vinum tuum."

Suddenly, Spectrum appears before Gaius, full of laughter. "You found me, Gaius! Take your wine."

Interea, supra in palatio, legatus suum vinum desiderat. "Vinum meum pretiosum ubi est?" alta voce clamat.

Meanwhile, above in the palace, the ambassador desires his wine. "Where is my precious wine?" he shouts loudly.

Gaius, vinum tenens, Spectrum criminatur. "Tu hoc egisti! Nunc legatus iratus est."

Gaius, holding the wine, blames Spectrum. "You did this! Now the ambassador is angry."

Invisibilis praeter Gaium, Spectrum ad legatum accedit et, quasi ex nihilo, vinum restituit.

Invisible beside Gaius, Spectrum approaches the ambassador and, as if from nowhere, returns the wine.

Legatus, vinum subito inveniens, miratur sed laetatur. "Vinum meum! Quomodo hoc factum est?"

The ambassador, suddenly finding the wine, is amazed but pleased. "My wine! How did this happen?"

Gaius, conversus ad Spectrum, gratias agit. "Tibi gratias ago, Spectrum, sed victoria adhuc mihi est petenda."

Gaius, turning to Spectrum, gives thanks. "Thank you, Spectrum, but I still have to claim victory."

Spectrum, cogitans de arte nova, ludum sequentem suggerit. "Paratus es, Gaie? Progredimur in nostro ludo."

Spectrum, thinking of a new trick, suggests the next game. "Are you ready, Gaius? We continue our game."

Et sic, intra muros palatii Romani, servus et spiritus ludicrus ad novas nocturnasque machinationes invicem provocantur, aleam vinariam inter se iocantes.

And thus, within the walls of the Roman palace, the servant and the playful spirit challenge each other to new nocturnal schemes, playfully wagering wine between them.

Fabula Evasiva

Spectrum, cum risu callido, Gaium provocat: "Gaie, audesne aliquid pretiosum legati occultare?"

The spirit, with a sly laugh, challenges Gaius: "Gaius, do you dare to hide something valuable from the ambassador?"

Gaius, cupiditate provocatus, anulum legati magni pretii furtim capit. "Ecce, Spectrum, anulum legati habeo!"

Gaius, driven by greed, secretly takes the ambassador's valuable ring. "Look, Spectrum, I have the ambassador's ring!"

Legatus, anulum suum desiderans, convivium magnum parat. "Ubi est anulus meus?" frequenter interrogat.

The ambassador, wanting his ring back, prepares a great banquet. "Where is my ring?" he frequently asks.

Gaius, locum secretum quaerens, non animadvertit Spectrum sequentem. Spectrum, arte sua usus, anulum in loco impossibili collocat.

Gaius, searching for a secret hiding place, does not notice Spectrum following him. Spectrum, using his magic, places the ring in an impossible location.

Legatus, anulo amisso, vehementer irascitur. "Quis anulum meum abstulit?" clamat.

The ambassador, having lost his ring, becomes very angry. "Who stole my ring?" he shouts.

Gaius et Spectrum, simul anulum quaerentes, in ludum intensiorem incidunt. Spectrum, Gaium subtiliter adiuvans, tamen de difficultate eius ridet.

Gaius and Spectrum, searching for the ring together, find themselves in an intense game. Spectrum, subtly helping Gaius, nevertheless laughs at his difficulty.

Mirum in modum, anulus in capsa Gaii invenitur. "Quomodo hic venit?" Gaius sibi ipse miratur.

Miraculously, the ring is found in Gaius' box. "How did it get here?" Gaius wonders to himself.

Legatus, anulum inventum laudans, Gaium honorat. "Gaie, servus fidelis, quam peritus es!"

The ambassador, praising the found ring, honors Gaius. "Gaius, faithful servant, how skilled you are!"

Gaius, interius Spectrum gratias agens, tamen sibi laudem arrogat. "Ego semper solutio sum," fidenter inquit.

Gaius, inwardly thanking Spectrum, nevertheless takes the credit for himself. "I am always the solution," he says confidently.

Spectrum, novum dolum meditans, ad proximum ludum se parat. "Gaie, paratusne es adhuc ludere?" subridet.

Spectrum, planning a new trick, prepares for the next game. "Gaius, are you still ready to play?" he grins.

Cum convivio in pleno esse, anulus ostentatur, et Gaius, propter inventum, popularis efficitur. Sed cautus manet, Spectrum dolos metuens.

With the banquet in full swing, the ring is displayed, and Gaius becomes popular because of its recovery. But he remains cautious, fearing Spectrum's tricks.

"Spectrum, novum ludum incipiamus," Gaius provocat, spiritum ludendi numquam amittens.

"Spectrum, let's start a new game," Gaius challenges, never losing his playful spirit.

Et sic, inter risus et mysteria palatii Romani, servus et spectrum in ludo et amicitia profundiore se involvunt, semper alter alterum in novis artibus provocantes.

And so, amidst the laughter and mysteries of the Roman palace, the servant and the spirit become more deeply involved in their game and friendship, always challenging each other with new tricks.

Convivii Perturbatio

In nocte convivii magni, Spectrum, spiritus ludicrus, turbationem memorabilem parare statuit. "Hac nocte, Gaie," Spectrum dicit, "convivium inauditum faciemus."

On the night of the grand banquet, Spectrum, the mischievous spirit, decides to prepare a memorable disruption. "Tonight, Gaius," says Spectrum, "we will make an unforgettable feast."

Gaius, inter parationes convivii occupatus, consilium Spectrum audit et subridet. "Bene, videamus quas nugas habes," Gaius respondet.

Gaius, busy with the banquet preparations, listens to Spectrum's plan and smiles. "Well, let's see what tricks you have," Gaius replies.

Convivae, eleganter vestiti, adveniunt, omnia in palatio regaliter ornata. Subito, Spectrum lucernas extinguere et ventos magicos vocare decernit, tenebris et sonis subitis omnes terrifacit.

The guests, elegantly dressed, arrive, and the palace is decorated in royal splendor. Suddenly, Spectrum decides to extinguish the lamps and summon magical winds, frightening everyone with darkness and sudden noises.

"Haec domus maleficata videtur!" convivae susurrant, perterriti, dum Gaius, cachinnans, conatur lumina restituere.

"This house seems cursed!" the guests whisper, terrified, while Gaius, laughing, tries to restore the lights.

Dum Gaius ad lumina reparanda laborat, Spectrum apparitiones metuendas creat, convivarum terrorem augens.

While Gaius works to fix the lights, Spectrum creates terrifying apparitions, increasing the guests' fear.

Legatus, suum convivium periclitari videns, exclamat, "Hoc spectrum exorcizare debemus!"

The ambassador, seeing his banquet in danger, exclaims, "We must exorcise this specter!"

Intellecto ludo spectri, Gaius cum Spectrum colludere statuit, convivium sub hora critica salvans. Lumina restituuntur, et Spectrum desinit ne convivae ulterius terreat.

Realizing Spectrum's game, Gaius decides to collaborate with him, saving the banquet at a critical moment. The lights are restored, and Spectrum stops frightening the guests further.

Legatus, convivium salvatum videns, se risui dat et convivas delectat, "Fortitudo Romana nos servavit!" exclamat.

The ambassador, seeing the banquet saved, bursts into laughter and entertains the guests, exclaiming, "Roman strength has saved us!"

Convivae, tandem securi, risu solvuntur, nocturnos terrores ludicre narrantes, audacter "larvam" palatii laudantes.

The guests, now safe, break into laughter, humorously recounting the night's terrors and boldly praising the palace's "ghost."

Gaius, credens se Spectrum superavisse, victoriam sibi arrogat. "Semper te superabo," Gaius Spectrum dicit, ridens.

Gaius, believing he has outwitted Spectrum, claims victory for himself. "I will always beat you," Gaius says, laughing.

Spectrum, non victa sed ad nova consilia inspirata, susurrat, "Ludus noster adhuc non finitur."

Spectrum, not defeated but inspired for new tricks, whispers, "Our game is not over yet."

Convivio ad finem veniente, omnes, vino et hilaritate repleti, discedunt, legatus imprimis Gaium laudans pro eius "fortitudine" contra supernaturalia.

As the banquet comes to an end, everyone, filled with wine and laughter, departs, with the ambassador especially praising Gaius for his "bravery" against the supernatural.

Et ita, servus et larva ludicra non solum ludi sed etiam amicitiae paginae novas in historia palatii Romani Londinii scribunt.

And so, the clever servant and the mischievous ghost continue to write new chapters not only of games but also of friendship in the history of the Roman palace in London.

Nuntius Phantasmatis

In palatio legati, Spectrum, spiritus ludicrus, audacem consilium capit: nuntium falsum ad legatum mittit. "Gaie, hunc nuntium ad legatum porta," inquit, papyrum ridiculam in manibus tenens.

In the ambassador's palace, Spectrum, the mischievous spirit, devises a bold plan: he sends a fake message to the ambassador. "Gaius, take this message to the ambassador," he says, holding a ridiculous scroll in his hands.

Gaius, nuntium legens, perplexus est. "Verba haec absurda sunt! Num legatus his credet?" dubitat.

Gaius, reading the message, is puzzled. "These words are absurd! Will the ambassador believe this?" he doubts.

Legatus, nuntium accipiens, statim fallaciam detegit. "Spectrum ludibrium hoc est," submurmurat.

The ambassador, receiving the message, immediately detects the trick. "This is Spectrum's mischief," he mutters.

Certamen inter Gaium et Spectrum incipit. "Quid semper me in tuas nugas implicare vis?" Gaius reclamat.

A quarrel begins between Gaius and Spectrum. "Why do you always want to involve me in your pranks?" Gaius protests.

Tum Spectrum, magica arte usus, legato epistulam luce coruscantem demonstrat. "Ecce, nuntium mirabilem," dicit.

Then Spectrum, using magical art, shows the ambassador a letter shining with light. "Behold, a wondrous message," he says.

Legatus, epistulae magicae ductus, inceptum sequitur et mox in casum inopinatum et ridiculum cadit. "Incredibile," exclamat, cum se in rerum confusionem invenit.

The ambassador, led by the magical letter, follows the course and soon finds himself in an unexpected and ridiculous situation. "Incredible," he exclaims, as he finds himself in a mess.

Gaius, cernens quid acciderit, ridet, sed legatus, ira commotus, inquirit, "Quis ausus est hoc facere?"

Gaius, seeing what has happened, laughs, but the ambassador, moved by anger, asks, "Who dared to do this?"

Spectrum, ne legatus ira consumatur, apparuit et veritatem profert. "Ego hoc feci, Spectrum, spiritus tuus fidelis," fatetur.

Spectrum, to prevent the ambassador from being consumed by anger, appears and tells the truth. "I did this, Spectrum, your loyal spirit," he admits.

Legatus, Spectrum ingenium laudans, cautionem tamen offert. "Ludi tui ingeniosi sunt, Spectrum, sed ne ultra fas agas."

The ambassador, praising Spectrum's cleverness, offers a warning. "Your games are ingenious, Spectrum, but don't go too far."

Gaius, adhuc indignans, Spectrum obiurgat. "Noli me tamquam pilam in ludis tuis habere!"

Gaius, still indignant, scolds Spectrum. "Don't use me as a pawn in your games!"

Spectrum, sentiens Gaii offensionem, paenitet et reconciliari vult. "Gaie, ignosce mihi. Possumusne amici esse iterum?"

Spectrum, feeling Gaius' offense, regrets it and wants to reconcile. "Gaius, forgive me. Can we be friends again?"

Legatus, audita eorum reconciliatione, gaudet et novam ideam proponit. "Quid si ambo in ludo mecum partem capiatis?"

The ambassador, hearing their reconciliation, is pleased and proposes a new idea. "What if both of you join me in a game?"

Concordia inter eos fit, et sic nova societas incipit. Legatus fabulas de spiritibus et servis antiquis palatii narrat.

Harmony is restored between them, and so a new partnership begins. The ambassador tells stories of spirits and ancient servants of the palace.

Gaius et Spectrum, nunc magis coniuncti, ad novas provocationes se praeparant. "In hoc simul sumus," Gaius confirmat.

Gaius and Spectrum, now closer, prepare themselves for new challenges. "We're in this together," Gaius affirms.

Inter ludos et secreta, amicitia inter Gaium servum et Spectrum in palatio Londiniensi floret, novas historias et memorabiles momentos creans.

Amid games and secrets, the friendship between Gaius the servant and Spectrum flourishes in the London palace, creating new stories and memorable moments.

Inquisitio Thesauri

Legatus, palatii mysterium augens, magnam proclamationem facit: thesaurum antiquum intra palatii muros absconditum esse nuntiat. "Audite, Gaie et Spectrum," inquit, "magnus thesaurus hic in palatio celatus est."

The ambassador, heightening the mystery of the palace, makes a great proclamation: he announces that an ancient treasure is hidden within the walls of the palace. "Listen, Gaius and Spectrum," he says, "a great treasure is hidden here in the palace."

Audita hac novitate, Spectrum et Gaius intuitus inter se coniungunt. "Eamus et quaeramus!" exclamat Spectrum. "Simul," Gaius assentit.

Upon hearing this news, Spectrum and Gaius exchange glances. "Let's go and search for it!" exclaims Spectrum. "Together," Gaius agrees.

Secundum legati narrationem, pericula et indicia per totum palatium dispersa sunt. Spectrum, secretis viarum gnarus, aditus occultos et cryptas revelat.

According to the ambassador's account, dangers and clues are scattered throughout the palace. Spectrum, familiar with the secret ways, reveals hidden passages and crypts.

Confisi in ingenium Gaii et in potestatem magicam Spectri, tandem aditum ad cryptam subterraneam inveniunt. Sed, o sorte! Ingressus obstaculo valvae fortiter clausus est.

Relying on Gaius' cleverness and Spectrum's magical power, they finally find the entrance to an underground crypt. But, alas! The entrance is firmly blocked by a gate.

"Spectrum, hanc valvam transire potes?" Gaius interrogat. Spectrum, natura sua levi et soluta utitur, faciliter transgreditur, sed Gaius coram enigmate constitit.

"Gaius, can you pass through this gate?" Gaius asks. Spectrum, using his light and fluid nature, easily passes through, but Gaius is faced with a riddle.

Manibus coniunctis, enigma solvunt, et post multos conatus, locum thesauri attingunt. Sed quid inveniunt? Arcula aperta, intus autem vacuitas.

With their hands joined, they solve the riddle, and after many efforts, they reach the location of the treasure. But what do they find? The chest is open, but inside, it is empty.

In fundo arcae, inscriptio parva in tabula reperitur: "Verus thesaurus in amicitia est." Gaius et Spectrum, quamvis primo frustrati, mox in risum erumpunt.

At the bottom of the chest, they find a small inscription on a plaque: "The true treasure is in friendship." Although initially disappointed, Gaius and Spectrum soon burst into laughter.

Legatus, subito apparuens, sapientiam eorum laudat. "Intelligitis," ait, "veras divitias in amicitia et amore, non in auro, consistere."

The ambassador, suddenly appearing, praises their wisdom. "You understand," he says, "that true wealth lies in friendship and love, not in gold."

Reflexi super lusus et certamina praeterita, Gaius et Spectrum de futuro consociato deliberant. "Non sumus adversarii, sed socii," Gaius pronuntiat.

Reflecting on past games and challenges, Gaius and Spectrum discuss their shared future. "We are not rivals, but partners," Gaius declares.

Legatus, eorum consensu audito, exsultat et prandium opulentum promittit. "Optime fecistis, et hic est vestra merces."

The ambassador, hearing their agreement, rejoices and promises a grand feast. "You have done well, and here is your reward."

Illa nocte, celebratio magna in palatio fit, ubi risus, musica, et gaudium regnant.

That night, a great celebration takes place in the palace, where laughter, music, and joy reign.

Gaius et Spectrum, iam non tantum socii sed etiam amici veri, de futuris schematibus et conatibus communi mente meditantur.

Gaius and Spectrum, now not just partners but true friends, ponder future schemes and endeavors with shared minds.

Finis advenit diei pleni mysteriis et amicitiae, ubi servus et spectrum, per venationem thesauri, aliquid longe pretiosius inveniunt: profundam et sinceram amicitiam inter se.

The day, full of mysteries and friendship, comes to an end, where the servant and the spirit, through their treasure hunt, find something far more precious: a deep and genuine friendship between them.

Confrontatio

Spectrum et Gaius, ultimum eorum ludum parantes, statuunt se palatium legati defendere. "Hoc palatium tutabimur, quasi nostrum esset," inquit Spectrum.

The spirit and Gaius, preparing their final game, decide to defend the ambassador's palace. "We will protect this palace as if it were our own," says the spirit.

Nocte obscura, latrones audaces muros palatii transcendere conantur, non simplicem thesaurum, sed aliquid longe pretiosius quaerentes.

On a dark night, bold thieves attempt to climb the palace walls, seeking not a simple treasure, but something far more precious.

Consilium inter se capientes, Gaius et Spectrum machinationes subdolas disponunt. "In laqueos eos ducemus," Gaius affirmat, instrumenta varia et retia parans.

After consulting with each other, Gaius and the spirit set up cunning traps. "We will lead them into snares," Gaius affirms, preparing various tools and nets.

Utentes magia, Spectrum phantasmata terribilia creat, quae latrones per umbras palatii persequuntur et in formidinem agunt.

Using magic, the spirit creates terrifying phantoms, which chase the thieves through the shadows of the palace, filling them with fear.

Incidunt latrones in praeparatas insidias, omnes praeter unum, qui calliditate sua effugit. "Sequere illum, Spectrum! Ego legatum certiorem faciam," Gaius exclamat, planum divisum proponens.

The thieves fall into the prepared traps, all except one, who escapes by his cunning. "Follow him, Spirit! I will inform the ambassador," Gaius shouts, proposing a split plan.

Latro, in profundam cryptam se abdens, falsa fiducia deceptus est, nam illic Spectrum, non thesaurum, occurrit. Spectrum, vi sua magica utens, formam terribilem assumit, ultimamque formidinem in latronem infundit.

The thief, hiding in a deep crypt, is deceived by false confidence, for there he encounters the spirit, not the treasure. The spirit, using his magical power, takes on a terrifying form and instills ultimate fear in the thief.

Gaius, cum legato et custodibus veniens, latrones in vincula conicit. "Capti sunt omnes," victoriae clamorem tollit.

Gaius, arriving with the ambassador and the guards, captures the thieves. "They are all caught," he shouts in victory.

Legatus, actus heroicos Gaii et Spectrum spectans, profundo eis gratias agit. "Vos, sine dubio, veri protectores huius loci estis," eos ut heroes palatii celebrans.

The ambassador, witnessing the heroic deeds of Gaius and the spirit, offers them profound thanks. "Without a doubt, you are the true protectors of this place," he says, celebrating them as the palace's heroes.

Magnae celebrationes fiunt, ubi Gaius et Spectrum, ob egregias res gestas, summo honore afficiuntur. Convivium resonat musica et gaudio repletur.

Great celebrations are held, where Gaius and the spirit are honored for their outstanding deeds. The banquet resonates with music and is filled with joy.

Dum convivium procedit, Spectrum momento gravi legato veram suam naturam aperit. "Spiritus amicus sum, pacemque hic quaero."

As the banquet continues, the spirit, in a solemn moment, reveals his true nature to the ambassador. "I am a friendly spirit, and I seek peace here."

Cum finis appropinquat, Gaius et Spectrum, futura meditantes, pacem et ludos novos somniant. "Futura incerta sunt, sed parati ad quidquid veniet, una stabimus," Spectrum suaviter dicit.

As the end approaches, Gaius and the spirit, contemplating the future, dream of peace and new games. "The future is uncertain, but whatever comes, we will stand together," the spirit says softly.

Ita finitur narratio, ubi Gaius et Spectrum, amicitia et laetitia pleni, palatii angulos custodiunt, parati ad proximas quaslibet periculas, nunc amicis firmioribus quam unquam ante.

Thus the story ends, where Gaius and the spirit, full of friendship and joy, guard the corners of the palace, ready for any future dangers, now closer friends than ever before.

Umbrae Templi Baalis

In Mesopotamiam Veniunt

Tres legati Romani, Marcus, Quintus et Gaius, Mesopotamiam petunt. Amici firmi et milites audaces, terram antiquam ac mysteriis plenam exploraturi sunt.

Three Roman envoys, Marcus, Quintus, and Gaius, head to Mesopotamia. They are steadfast friends and brave soldiers, about to explore an ancient and mystery-filled land.

Iter per silvas densas montesque arduos aggrediuntur. Nocte, sub sideribus claris, castra figunt et ad ignem fabulas narrare incipiunt.

They embark on a journey through dense forests and steep mountains. At night, under the bright stars, they set up camp and begin to tell stories by the fire.

"Num de templo Baalis aliquid audistis?" Quintus rogat. "Fama est spiritum malignum illic habitare."

"Have you heard anything about the Temple of Baal?" Quintus asks. "Rumor has it that an evil spirit dwells there."

Marcus, vir fortitudine conspicuus, respondet: "Fabulae sunt, nihil amplius, quae milites terrendos parant."

Marcus, a man known for his strength, responds, "They are just stories, nothing more, meant to scare soldiers."

Gaius autem ridet: "Spiritus me non terrent. Fortes sumus!"

But Gaius laughs, "Spirits don't scare me. We are strong!"

Cum lux oritur, ad vetustum templum perveniunt, cuius portae horrendae eos excipiunt. "Hoc loco... malum quoddam inest," Quintus submisse dicit.

As dawn breaks, they arrive at the ancient temple, whose dreadful gates greet them. "There is something evil in this place..." Quintus murmurs softly.

Moenia templi intrant, ubi frigus insolitum sentiunt. Statuae deorum, oculis inanibus, eos circumstant.

They enter the walls of the temple, where they feel an unusual chill. Statues of gods with empty eyes surround them.

"Num hic manere oportet?" Gaius, nunc minus audax, interrogat.

"Should we stay here?" Gaius, now less bold, asks.

"Explorandum est," Marcus asserit. "Forsitan aliquid utile inveniemus."

"We must explore," Marcus insists. "Perhaps we will find something useful."

Verum intra templi parietes, non thesauros, sed arcana inveniunt. Voces susurrantes audiuntur, et frigidae aurae eos ambiunt.

But within the temple's walls, they find not treasures, but secrets. Whispering voices are heard, and cold breezes surround them.

"Quid agendum est?" Quintus, timore affectus, rogat. "Hoc loco aliquid prorsus diversum inest."

"What should we do?" Quintus, affected by fear, asks. "There is something entirely different in this place."

Gaius, paululum sollicitus, suadet: "Fortasse hinc discedere melius est."

Gaius, now slightly worried, suggests, "Perhaps it's better if we leave."

Sed sero iam est. Quidam vis invisibilis eos detinet, et sic fabula incipit. Armis amicitiaeque praediti, tres amici mysterium templi antiqui solvere conantur. Sed spiritus malignus non facile superatur.

But it is already too late. An invisible force holds them back, and thus the story begins. Armed with friendship and courage, the three friends attempt to solve the mystery of the ancient temple. But the evil spirit is not easily defeated.

Spiritus Excitatur

In medio templi, altare magnum obscurumque deprehendunt. Marcus, rerum novarum cupidus, ad altare accedit et anulum antiquum conspicit.

In the middle of the temple, they discover a large and dark altar. Marcus, eager for new discoveries, approaches the altar and notices an ancient ring.

"En! Anulus antiquus!" Marcus exclamat, anulum tollens. Statim, ventus frigidus inexplicabiliter oritur.

"Look! An ancient ring!" Marcus exclaims, picking up the ring. Immediately, a cold wind inexplicably arises.

Lucernae repente extinguuntur, tenebris cuncta obvelantibus. "Quidnam hoc est?" Gaius, tremore affectus, inquirit, vocem lugubrem audiens.

The lamps suddenly go out, covering everything in darkness. "What is happening?" Gaius, trembling, asks, hearing a mournful voice.

"Spiritus hoc effecit!" Quintus, timore plenus, susurrat. "Anulum sustulisti et spiritum excitavimus!"

"The spirit did this!" Quintus, full of fear, whispers. "You took the ring and we have awakened the spirit!"

Statuae, prius immobiles, nunc quasi ad motum venire incipiunt. Marcus, anulum manu tenens, errorem suum agnoscit.

The statues, previously motionless, now seem to begin moving. Marcus, holding the ring in his hand, recognizes his mistake.

"Restitue!" inquit, anulum in altare reponere conans. Sed anulus loco non movetur.

"Return it!" he says, trying to put the ring back on the altar. But the ring does not move from its place.

"Fugere oportet!" Marcus clamat. Sed ad portas festinantes, eas clausas inveniunt.

"We must flee!" Marcus shouts. But when they rush to the doors, they find them closed.

Voces lamentationesque in tenebris crescunt. Subito, pallida lumina apparent, spiritum formam horrendam induentia.

The voices and wailing in the darkness grow louder. Suddenly, pale lights appear, forming a terrifying shape of the spirit.

Lapis, sine ullius manus iactu, Gaium ferit. "Quis me lapidavit?" exclamat, neminem conspicatus.

A stone, thrown by no hand, hits Gaius. "Who stoned me?" he shouts, seeing no one.

Amici, metu oppleti, in angulum templi confugiunt. "Quid agemus?" Gaius rogat.

The friends, overwhelmed by fear, retreat to a corner of the temple. "What will we do?" Gaius asks.

Nocte, conati dormire, ab spiritu territantur. Somnia terribilia patiuntur, spiritu eos inquietante.

At night, trying to sleep, they are terrified by the spirit. They endure terrible dreams, disturbed by the spirit.

"Nequam hoc est," Quintus in somnis loquitur. "Huc venire non oportuit."

"This is wicked," Quintus speaks in his sleep. "We should not have come here."

"Cras," Marcus respondet, "exitum quaeremus." Sed illa nocte, verus somnus nemini datur. Spiritus, iam plene excitatus, incessanter eos vexat.

"Tomorrow," Marcus responds, "we will search for a way out." But that night, no true sleep comes to any of them. The spirit, now fully awakened, torments them without end.

Fuga Desperata

Mane orto, Marcus, Quintus et Gaius consilium capiunt de templo exeundi. "Exire debemus, amici," inquit Marcus, anulum gestans.

At dawn, Marcus, Quintus, and Gaius make the decision to leave the temple. "We must leave, my friends," says Marcus, holding the ring.

In templo murum occultum deprehendunt. "Ecce!" exclamat Quintus. "Forte hinc evadere possumus." Laboribus magnis viam aperiunt; iter angustum et obscurum se praebet.

In the temple, they discover a hidden wall. "Look!" Quintus exclaims. "Perhaps we can escape this way." With great effort, they open a path; a narrow and dark passage is revealed.

"Hac nobis eundum est," Marcus praeeunte dicit. Per angustias et tenebras progrediuntur, susurros audiunt.

"We must go this way," says Marcus, leading the way. They proceed through the narrow space and darkness, hearing whispers.

Repente in labyrinthum subterraneum devolvuntur. "Quo loco sumus?" Gaius susurrans quaerit.

Suddenly, they find themselves in an underground labyrinth. "Where are we?" Gaius whispers, asking.

"Prudentes simus," Quintus admonet, "fama est mihi de huiuscemodi locis." Marcus, lumen praeferens, semper anteit.

"Let's be cautious," Quintus warns, "I've heard stories about places like this." Marcus, holding the light, always moves ahead.

Terra mox tremere incipit. "Fugite!" clamat Marcus, cadentibus lapidibus vitatis.

Soon, the ground begins to shake. "Run!" shouts Marcus, avoiding the falling stones.

Cameram sarcophagis plenam inveniunt. Sarcophagi aperiuntur, et ex eis umbrae surgunt.

They find a chamber full of sarcophagi. The sarcophagi open, and shadows rise from them.

"Quid petunt?" Gaius clamat, umbrae clamantes audientes. "Vindictam... aequitatem..." umbrae susurrant.

"What do they want?" Gaius shouts, hearing the wailing shadows. "Vengeance... justice..." the shadows whisper.

"Non licet nobis hic manere," statuit Marcus. Persequuntur viam, umbrae eos insecutae.

"We cannot stay here," Marcus decides. They follow the path, with the shadows pursuing them.

Exitum tandem inveniunt, sed magno lapide obstructum. "Movendum est hoc!" Gaius, adiuvans Marcum, Quintus incantationes profert.

They finally find an exit, but it is blocked by a large stone. "We must move this!" Gaius says, helping Marcus, while Quintus chants incantations.

Magna cum strepitu lapis movetur. Lux inrumpit, eorum oculos feriens. Effugiunt, spiritu adhuc invisibili eos sequente.

With a great noise, the stone is moved. Light bursts in, blinding their eyes. They escape, with the invisible spirit still following them.

"Secum manet," Quintus suspirat, templum egredientes.

"It stays with us," Quintus sighs, as they leave the temple.

Ad castra redire, turbati sed salvi, anulum portantes. "Quid agendum?" Gaius rogat, in ignem intentus.

They return to the camp, shaken but safe, carrying the ring. "What should we do?" Gaius asks, staring into the fire.

"Id nescio," Marcus respondet, anulum spectans. "Verum remedium invenire oportet." Illa nocte, cogitationibus de futuro pressi, in castris manent.

"I don't know," Marcus replies, gazing at the ring. "We must find the true remedy." That night, weighed down by thoughts of the future, they remain in the camp.

Maledictio Perseverat

Cum ad castra revertuntur, Marcus, Quintus et Gaius desolationem inveniunt. "Quo omnes abierunt?" Gaius circumspiciens rogat.

When they return to the camp, Marcus, Quintus, and Gaius find desolation. "Where has everyone gone?" Gaius asks, looking around.

Nocte, visiones horrendas patiuntur, templi ruinis mortisque plenas. "Spiritus nobiscum loquitur," Quintus somnians susurrat.

At night, they suffer horrible visions, filled with ruins of the temple and death. "The spirit speaks to us," Quintus whispers in his sleep.

Prima luce, Marcus anulum in silvam abicere conatur, sed mirum in modum ad eum revertitur. "Quae res est haec?" exclamat, anulum inspectans.

At first light, Marcus tries to throw the ring into the forest, but, miraculously, it returns to him. "What is this?" he exclaims, inspecting the ring.

Quintus in antiquis scriptis remedium quaerit. "Nihil reperio," frustratus ait.

Quintus searches for a remedy in ancient texts. "I find nothing," he says in frustration.

Gaius subito aegrotare incipit, pallens et febricitans. "Quid mihi accidit?" infirma voce queritur.

Gaius suddenly falls ill, pale and feverish. "What is happening to me?" he asks in a weak voice.

In silvis, voces mortuorum audiri incipiunt, sua nomina vocantes. "Nos vocant," Marcus, timore affectus, susurrat.

In the woods, voices of the dead begin to be heard, calling their names. "They are calling us," Marcus whispers, filled with fear.

Cibus aquaque in castris sine causa corrumpuntur. "Quid agemus?" Gaius ex desperatione rogat.

The food and water in the camp spoil without reason. "What will we do?" Gaius asks in desperation.

Etiam silvae animalia, tamquam maledictionem percipientia, eos vitant. "Discede!" lupus in vicinia latrat, sed non appropinquat.

Even the animals of the forest, as if sensing the curse, avoid them. "Go away!" a wolf barks nearby but does not approach.

Nuntios ad alios Romanos mittunt, sed nullus revertitur. "Relicti sumus," Quintus capite demisso dicit.

They send messages to other Romans, but no one returns. "We are abandoned," Quintus says with his head down.

Spiritus in somniis apparet, anuli redditionem exigens. "Quid desiderat?" Gaius, tremens, interrogat.

The spirit appears in dreams, demanding the return of the ring. "What does it want?" Gaius asks, trembling.

Subito, tempestas horrenda surgit, fulminibus et ventis vehementibus. "Spiritus hoc efficit," Marcus, procellae resistens, clamat.

Suddenly, a terrible storm arises, with lightning and violent winds. "The spirit is causing this," Marcus shouts, resisting the storm.

Noctu, umbrae castra circumvolant, lumen nocturnum exstinguunt. "Ecce!" Quintus adumbrationes indicans exclamat.

At night, shadows fly around the camp, extinguishing the moonlight. "Look!" Quintus exclaims, pointing at the shadows.

Desperatione actus, Marcus anulum in proximum flumen proicit. Anulo demisso, tempestas statim cessat.

In desperation, Marcus throws the ring into the nearest river. As the ring sinks, the storm immediately stops.

Verum, tempestate desistente, Marcus in aquam trahitur. "Marcus!" Gaius clamat, sed amicus iam evanuit.

However, as the storm ceases, Marcus is pulled into the water. "Marcus!" Gaius shouts, but his friend has already disappeared.

Quintus et Gaius, soli superstiti et maledictione gravati, invicem aspiciunt. "Quid faciemus?" Quintus, de amico et anulo amissis, inquit.

Quintus and Gaius, the only survivors and burdened by the curse, look at each other. "What will we do?" Quintus asks, mourning the loss of their friend and the ring.

Finis Maledicti

Gravati animo et futuro incerto, Quintus et Gaius consilia graviora capiunt. "Necesse est ad templum redire," Quintus firmiter dicit. "Forsitan ibi responsum reperiemus, quid agendum sit."

Weighed down with heavy hearts and uncertain about the future, Quintus and Gaius make a serious decision. "It is necessary to return to the temple," Quintus says firmly. "Perhaps there we will find the answer to what must be done."

Nocte iter arduum et trepidum ad templi ruinas incipiunt. Luna pallida vix viam illuminat, spiritus montis susurros subtiliter emittunt, qui viatores nostros quasi vento gelido tangunt. Ubi ad templi ruinas perveniunt, Quintus et Gaius locum, qui olim terrore plenus erat, nunc miram quietem prae se ferre vident.

At night, they begin their difficult and fearful journey to the ruins of the temple. The pale moon barely illuminates the path, and the spirits of the mountain emit subtle whispers that touch our travelers like a cold wind. When they reach the ruins of the temple, Quintus and Gaius see that the place, once full of terror, now carries an eerie calm.

In mediis ruinis, ad altare fractum, consistunt. "Circumspiciamus," Quintus suadet, dum tremulis manibus inter saxa et antiquas herbas scrutantur. Nullum anuli signum inveniunt, sed subito clamores exanimatos audiunt, non tam terribiles quam antea, sed potius quasi voces alios viatores ad locum invitant.

In the middle of the ruins, they stop at the broken altar. "Let's search around," Quintus suggests, as they nervously sift through the rocks and ancient plants with trembling hands. They find no sign of the ring, but suddenly they hear eerie cries—not as terrifying as before, but more like voices inviting other travelers to the place.

His vocibus ducti, ad templi partem alteram procedunt, ubi turba parva viatorum ex diversis terrarum orbis partibus collecta esse videtur. Hi viatores, mente capta et oculis vacuis, per templi ruinas vagantur, quasi somniantes.

Guided by these voices, they proceed to another part of the temple, where they see a small group of travelers seemingly gathered from different parts of the world. These travelers, with their minds entranced and eyes vacant, wander through the ruins of the temple as if in a dream.

Quintus et Gaius, sapientiores et cautiores, statim intellegunt hos viatores potestate maligna teneri, fortasse eodem spiritu qui Marcum traxit. "Non diutius hic morari possumus," Gaius murmure urget. "Ab hoc loco discedamus, priusquam et nos capiamur."

Quintus and Gaius, now wiser and more cautious, immediately understand that these travelers are being held by a malevolent force, possibly the same spirit that took Marcus. "We cannot stay here any longer," Gaius urges in a whisper. "Let us leave this place before we too are captured."

E loco celeriter exeunt, per silvas nocturnas retrorsum iter facientes. Dum redeunt, consilium formant quid in civitate faciendum sit.

They quickly exit the place, retracing their steps through the dark forest. As they return, they form a plan about what must be done when they reach the city.

Cum aurora appropinquat, silvae clarescunt et via aperitur. Quintus et Gaius, animo renovato, spem habent se, post haec pericula, responsa inventuros esse.

As dawn approaches, the forest brightens and the path clears. Quintus and Gaius, with renewed spirits, hope that after these dangers they will find the answers they seek.

Clavis Aeterni

In Umbra Mundi

Hades, rex inferorum, solus in solio suo sedet. Silentium umbrarum magni regni perturbatur. Per obscura regni spatia, animae mortuorum quae non quiescunt vagantur; murmur levis subter audiri potest. Inter has, Alecto, una ex potentioribus umbris, audax consilium cepit.

Hades, the king of the underworld, sits alone on his throne. The silence of the great kingdom of shadows is disturbed. Through the dark spaces of the realm, the restless souls of the dead wander; a faint murmur can be heard below. Among these, Alecto, one of the most powerful shadows, devised a bold plan.

Nocte quadam, sub pallida luce lunae infernae, Alecto ad umbras congregatas susurravit, "Fratres, diu in tenebris iacuimus, ignoti et oblivioni traditi. Videte, via ad vivos nos vocat. Necesse est nos fallere Hadem ut portas inferorum aperiat."

One night, under the pale light of the infernal moon, Alecto whispered to the gathered shadows, "Brothers, we have lain in darkness for too long, unknown and consigned to oblivion. Look, the way to the living calls to us. We must deceive Hades to open the gates of the underworld."

Umbrae, spem vix credentes, inter se murmurabant. "Sed quomodo? Portae clausae sunt, et Spiritus Antiquus, custos aeternus, claves tenet," una ex eis timide rogavit.

The shadows, barely daring to hope, murmured among themselves. "But how? The gates are closed, and the Ancient Spirit, the eternal guardian, holds the keys," one of them timidly asked.

"Sic," Alecto respondit, "artibus magicis et calliditate opus est. In regno Hadis, magicae artes vetitae sunt, verum in desperatione nostra, legem hanc frangere debemus."

"Thus," Alecto replied, "we need magic and cunning. In the kingdom of Hades, magical arts are forbidden, but in our desperation, we must break this law."

Dicto hoc, umbrae discere incantationes obscuras coeperunt. Hades, in alto solio residens, nihil de consiliis subter molientibus suspicabatur. Alecto, dux facta, multas umbras arte ductavit. "Nunc est tempus," inquit illa nocte, cum primum experimentum magicum tentarent. Sub furtiva nocte, arte magica sagitta prima emissa est, terram inferorum levi tremore concutiens.

With these words, the shadows began to learn dark incantations. Hades, sitting high on his throne, suspected nothing of the schemes brewing below. Alecto, having become their leader, guided many shadows with her craft. "Now is the time," she said that night, when they attempted their first magical experiment. Under the stealth of night, the first magical arrow was released, shaking the ground of the underworld with a faint tremor.

Hades, motu terrae excitatus, statim sensum pravitatis in aere sensit. "Quis hoc audet?" voce tonitrua in tenebras clamavit, sed nihil nisi silentium respondit.

Hades, awakened by the tremor, immediately sensed the foulness in the air. "Who dares this?" he thundered into the darkness, but nothing responded except silence.

Magicae Artis

Sub velamento noctis, umbrarum coetus in angulo obscuro regni inferorum convenit. Alecto, duce illarum, umbras magicae artis rudimenta docet. "Praestigia prima simplicia erunt," susurrat Alecto. Umbrae, discipuli intenti, in tenebris magicae voces repetunt.

Under the cover of night, a gathering of shadows meets in a dark corner of the underworld. Alecto, their leader, teaches them the basics of magical arts. "The first tricks will be simple," Alecto whispers. The shadows, attentive students, repeat the magical words in the darkness.

Nocte illa, cum luna pallide lucet, umbrae incantationes leniter susurrant. Terra subtiliter tremere incipit. Alecto, sensum periculi sentiens, umbras animat: "Ne cessate! Vim magicam augere debemus!"

That night, as the pale moon shines, the shadows softly whisper incantations. The ground begins to tremble slightly. Alecto, sensing danger, encourages the shadows: "Do not stop! We must strengthen the magic!"

Umbrae, magicae artis fiducia crescente, audacius incantant. Formae et imagines, similes hominibus vivis, ex nihilo surgere incipiunt. Haec simulacra, umbrae et fumus, per inferos vagari incipiunt, confundentes et terrentes inferorum incolas.

The shadows, growing in confidence with their magic, chant more boldly. Forms and images, resembling living humans, begin to arise from nothing. These apparitions, made of shadow and smoke, start to wander through the underworld, confusing and frightening its inhabitants.

Custos portarum, spiritus antiquus nomine Charon, somnia inquieta habet. Imagines turbatae eum ex somno excitant. "Quid hoc est? Num aliquid in regno meo geritur?" susurrat, somno confusus.

The gatekeeper, an ancient spirit named Charon, has restless dreams. Troubled visions wake him from sleep. "What is this? Is something happening in my realm?" he whispers, still dazed from sleep.

Alecto, occasione capta, ad Charontem accedit et sereno vultu loquitur, "Care Charon, te saluto! Quam bene te habes hac nocte?"

Seizing the opportunity, Alecto approaches Charon and speaks with a calm expression, "Dear Charon, I greet you! How well are you this night?"

Charon, cautus sed blanditiis mollitus, respondet, "Alecto, cur me in tenebris salutas? Somnia mala me vexant."

Charon, cautious but softened by flattery, responds, "Alecto, why do you greet me in the dark? Bad dreams trouble me."

"Somnia? Oh, noli sollicitari, fortasse umbras tantum vides," Alecto subdole respondet, cum mente aliam clavem portae subripiendi.

"Dreams? Oh, do not worry, perhaps you only see shadows," Alecto slyly responds, while secretly planning to steal another gate key.

Dum Charon somno rursus capitur, Alecto, manu tremula, lentissime ad cingulum eius manum porrigit, clavemque unam furtim extrahit. Umbras, quae procul stant et spectant, successu Alectonis exhilarantur.

While Charon falls back into sleep, Alecto, with a trembling hand, slowly reaches for his belt and stealthily removes one key. The shadows, standing at a distance and watching, are thrilled by Alecto's success.

Returning to the shadows, Alecto shows the key: "Behold, our path to freedom!" she exclaims. "But we still must learn more skills; Hades is already beginning to suspect us."

Hades, rex inferorum, vere perturbatus, aulam suam circumspectat. "Aliquid hic non recte geritur," inquit. "Magis ac magis in regno meo rem non rectam sentio."

Hades, the king of the underworld, truly disturbed, looks around his hall. "Something is not right here," he says. "More and more, I feel something is wrong in my realm."

Alecto, clam ad umbras congregatas: "Nunc magis quam umquam, artes nostras debemus firmare. Fortiores fieri debemus!"

Alecto, secretly addressing the gathered shadows: "Now more than ever, we must strengthen our skills. We must become stronger!"

Fallaciae Auctae

Alecto, umbrae dux, in secreto loco cum ceteris umbris convenit. Flammae exiguae lucis per tenebras sparguntur. "Audacius agere debemus," inquit Alecto. "Magis ac magis nostra arte utamur!"

Alecto, leader of the shadows, meets with the other shadows in a secret place. Tiny flames of light flicker through the darkness. "We must act more boldly," Alecto says. "Let us use our magic even more!"

Umbrae, ad consilium Alectonis allectae, potentes incantationes incipiunt. Manibus motis, formae horrendae et terribiles in aere formantur. "Ecce illusiones nostrae! Hac nocte, simulacra horrenda Hadem ipsum terrere temptabunt," Alecto pronuntiat.

The shadows, drawn by Alecto's plan, begin powerful incantations. With their hands moving, horrible and terrifying forms take shape in the air. "Behold our illusions! Tonight, we will try to terrify Hades himself with these dreadful apparitions," Alecto declares.

Noctu, cum luna abscondita sit, umbrae simulacra amentia in palatium regis mittunt. Hades, somno levi, subito expergefactus, simulacra, tam terribilia quam verba sine sonis, circumstantia videt.

At night, with the moon hidden, the shadows send their mad apparitions into the king's palace. Hades, lightly sleeping, suddenly awakens and sees the apparitions, as terrifying as silent words, surrounding him.

"Quid hoc est? Quae ista monstrorum forma?" Hades iratus clamat. Sed simulacra solum responsum silens offerunt, mox evanescunt.

"What is this? What are these monstrous forms?" Hades angrily shouts. But the apparitions offer only silent answers and soon disappear.

Hades, ira magna commotus, statim custodes suos convocat. "Custodes, vigilate! Aliquid pravum intra muros geritur," imperat Hades. Custodes armis et lanternis instructi per regnum circumeunt, sed nihil inveniunt.

Hades, greatly disturbed with anger, immediately summons his guards. "Guards, be vigilant! Something wicked is happening within these walls," Hades commands. The guards, equipped with weapons and lanterns, patrol the kingdom, but find nothing.

Interea, Alecto et umbrae vires suas colligunt pro magno impetu. In profundis regni angulis, magnum simulacrum, quod bellum inferorum simulare potest, moliri incipiunt. Alecto cunctis umbris praesentibus dicit, "Hoc erit opus nostrum maximum. Parate vos!"

Meanwhile, Alecto and the shadows gather their strength for a great assault. In the deep corners of the kingdom, they begin to create a giant apparition, capable of simulating a war in the underworld. Alecto, in the presence of all the shadows, says, "This will be our greatest work. Prepare yourselves!"

Omnes umbrae nocte illa ad locum secretum ab Alecto convocantur. Sub silentio lunae novae, simulacrum ingens, pulchrum sed horrendum, perficiunt. "Nunc, ad portas regis cum hoc monstrum ibimus!" Alecto excitata exclamat.

That night, all the shadows are summoned by Alecto to a secret place. Under the silence of the new moon, they complete the massive apparition, beautiful yet terrifying. "Now, we shall take this monster to the king's gates!" Alecto exclaims excitedly.

Umbrae, simulacrum ingens trahentes, tacite ad palatium Hadis procedunt. Hades, deceptione captus, simulacro se ipsum decipi permittit. "Quis vos misit? Quae haec vis nova?" Hades, confusus et territus, clamat.

The shadows, dragging the enormous apparition, silently proceed toward Hades' palace. Hades, caught in deception, allows himself to be fooled by the apparition. "Who sent you? What is this new power?" Hades, confused and terrified, shouts.

Simulacrum, ductum ab Alecto, Hadem ad veras portas inferorum ducit. Cum ad portas perveniunt, custos, qui ultimam clavem adhuc tenet, subito apparet. "Quid hic agitis? Non licet!" custos exclamat. Sed ante quam quid facere potest, umbrae portas pulsare incipiunt.

The apparition, led by Alecto, guides Hades to the real gates of the underworld. When they arrive at the gates, the guard, who still holds the last key, suddenly appears. "What are you doing here? This is forbidden!" the guard exclaims. But before he can act, the shadows begin pounding on the gates.

Hades, tandem fraude intellecta, ad veritatem revertit. "Fraus! Mea regna defendam!" clamat, sed iam ad portas inferorum stant, quae fere apertae sunt.

Hades, finally realizing the deception, returns to his senses. "Treachery! I will defend my realm!" he shouts, but they are already standing at the gates of the underworld, which are nearly opened.

Proelium in Umbra

Cum Hades simulacrum monstrum per tenebras sequeretur, subito veritatem deprehendit. Ira in corde suo ardet. "Quis hoc ausus est? Quae haec audacia est?" exclamat rex inferorum, vocem tonitrua similem effundens.

As Hades followed the monstrous apparition through the darkness, he suddenly realized the truth. Anger burns in his heart. "Who dared to do this? What is this audacity?" the king of the underworld exclaims, his voice thundering.

Umbrae, cum portas inferorum iam apertas viderent, magno impetu pugnare incipiunt. "Nunc aut numquam!" clamat Alecto, duce audaci. Magicae voces et gestus per aera volitant, potentes incantationes invocant.

The shadows, seeing the gates of the underworld already opened, begin to fight with great force. "Now or never!" shouts Alecto, their bold leader. Magical words and gestures fly through the air, invoking powerful spells.

Hades, contra Alectonem directus, manu valida fulmina coniurat. "Meos fines defendam!" vehementer clamat. Terra et aether toti tumultuantur, regnum inferorum quasi fundamentis suis moveri videtur.

Hades, facing Alecto, summons lightning with his strong hand. "I will defend my realm!" he shouts fiercely. Earth and sky are shaken; the entire underworld seems to tremble at its foundations.

Interea, custos, clavem ultimam tenens, magni periculi conscius, stat quid faciat deliberans. Dum tumultus crescit, clavem Hadi refert, "Domine, tene, ne omnia perdantur!" exclamat trepidus.

Meanwhile, the gatekeeper, holding the final key, aware of the great danger, stands deliberating what to do. As the chaos grows, he returns the key to Hades. "Master, take it, lest all be lost!" he cries, trembling.

Alecto, videns clavem ad Hadem reditam, desperat. "Fratres, sorores, ultimam vim nostram conemur!" incitat umbras. Sed iam debilitati sunt, viribus suis exhausti.

Alecto, seeing the key returned to Hades, despairs. "Brothers, sisters, let us try our final strength!" she urges the shadows. But they are already weakened, their power exhausted.

Hades, potentia sua maxima, magicae artes umbrarum reprimere incipit. Terra iterum quiescit, et Hades, "Satis est!" exclamat. Magna calamitas umbras occupat, quae sub magno Hade imperio nunc succumbunt.

Hades, with his immense power, begins to suppress the magic of the shadows. The earth grows still again, and Hades exclaims, "Enough!" A great calamity befalls the shadows, who now fall under the mighty dominion of Hades.

Ultimae spes Alectonis et umbrarum extinctae, portae inferorum magno sonitu clauduntur. Hades, nunc plenus irae et potestatis, severas poenas umbris imponit. "Pro audacia vestra, poenas graviores luetis!" Hades pronuntiat. Umbrae, vinculis invisibilibus restrictae, in tenebris aeternis recluduntur, ubi nullum lumen, nulla spes restat.

The last hopes of Alecto and the shadows are extinguished as the gates of the underworld close with a great sound. Hades, now full of wrath and power, imposes severe punishments on the shadows. "For your audacity, you will suffer the gravest penalties!" Hades declares. The shadows, bound by invisible chains, are imprisoned in eternal darkness, where no light or hope remains.

Silentium grave regnum inferorum nunc implet, umbraeque in perpetuum lamentantur, finem suae libertatis dolentes.

A heavy silence now fills the realm of the underworld, and the shadows mourn forever, lamenting the end of their freedom.

Caligo Aeterna

In profundo regni inferorum, umbrarum poenae aeternae perdurant. Alecto, catenis invisibilibus vincta, ad saxum frigidum appropinquat. Luctu maximo affecta, sussurrat, "Omnia perdita sunt. Spes nulla superest." Umbrarum gemitus per umbras diffunditur, quae iam nihil nisi desperatio tenet.

In the depths of the underworld, the eternal punishments of the shadows endure. Alecto, bound by invisible chains, approaches the cold stone. Overcome with great sorrow, she whispers, "All is lost. No hope remains." The groans of the shadows spread through the darkness, now held by nothing but despair.

Hades, rex victoriosus, imperium suum magis firmat. "Portas nostras munite," imperat custodibus, "nulla umbrarum fraus iterum nostrum regnum perturbet." Praesidia ad portas inferorum multiplicata sunt. Custodes, armis et luminibus nocturnis instructi, vigilant. Hades, in alto solio residens, regnum suum aspicit, oculos metus plenos habens ne iterum consilium contra se fiat.

Hades, the victorious king, strengthens his rule further. "Fortify our gates," he commands the guards, "let no shadow's trick ever again disturb our realm." The defenses at the gates of the underworld are increased. Guards, armed and equipped with nocturnal lights, stand watch. Hades, seated on his high throne, gazes over his realm, his eyes filled with the fear that another plot may rise against him.

"Numquam umbras magica uti sinemus," Hades clamat. Arte magica ex umbris extracta, amplius non licet in inferis. Alecto, omnium dolorum conscia, in angulum obscurum se recondit et sola relinquitur. "Libertas nostra, ut fumus, evanuit," murmure tristi inquit.

"We will never allow the shadows to use magic again," Hades declares. The magic is stripped from the shadows, no longer permitted in the underworld. Alecto, aware of all her suffering, hides herself in a dark corner and is left alone. "Our freedom, like smoke, has vanished," she says in a sorrowful murmur.

Tenebrae in regno densiores fiunt, et silentium profundum omnia implet. Regnum inferorum nunc quietum sed triste manet, nulla vox, nullus sonus laetitiae audiri potest. Custos portarum, vigilia perpetua, stationem suam nunquam deserit, lumen aeternum coram se portans.

The darkness in the kingdom grows thicker, and a deep silence fills everything. The underworld is now quiet but sad, no voice, no sound of joy can be heard. The gatekeeper, on eternal watch, never leaves his post, carrying an eternal light before him.

Hades, solio suo innixus, regnum suum regnat, nulla misericordia in corde. "Imperabo in aeternum," inquit, "nemo me superabit." Silentium aeternum nunc regnum inferorum regit, et Hades, rex implacabilis, sine fine dominatur. Umbrae in tenebris aeternis gemunt, finem libertatis dolentes, et spes omnis cum magica arte periit. In inferis, nihil nisi caligo aeterna et rex inexorabilis manent.

Hades, leaning on his throne, rules his realm with no mercy in his heart. "I will rule for eternity," he says, "no one will ever overcome me." Eternal silence now reigns over the underworld, and Hades, the implacable king, rules without end. The shadows groan in the eternal darkness, mourning the end of their freedom, and all hope perished with the magic. In the underworld, nothing remains but eternal gloom and an unyielding king.

Silvae Mysteria

Introductio

In antiqua villa Romana, homines felices habitant. Dominus villae, Gaius nomine, vir dives et potens est. Uxorem pulchram, Marciam, habet.

In an ancient Roman villa, happy people live. The master of the villa, named Gaius, is a wealthy and powerful man. He has a beautiful wife, Marcia.

Una nocte, Marcia somnium terribile videt et mane Gaium excitat. Marcia anxie dicit, "Gai, somnium horribile de spiritibus habui! Spiritus in silva nostra errare videntur!"

One night, Marcia has a terrible dream and wakes Gaius in the morning. Marcia anxiously says, "Gaius, I had a horrible dream about spirits! Spirits seem to wander in our forest!"

Gaius, qui somnia non timet, respondet, "O Marcia, somnia sunt somnia. Ne timeas."

Gaius, who does not fear dreams, responds, "Oh Marcia, dreams are just dreams. Do not be afraid."

Eodem tempore, filius eorum, Titus, et amicus eius, Lucius, parvi ad ianuam stant. Titus Lucium trahit et susurrat, "Veni, Luci! Nocte explorabimus!"

At the same time, their son, Titus, and his friend, Lucius, stand by the door. Titus pulls Lucius and whispers, "Come, Lucius! We will explore at night!"

Lucius, paulum timens, respondet, "In silvam? Sed mater tua..."

Lucius, a little afraid, replies, "Into the forest? But your mother..."

Titus ridet, "Ah, fabulae sunt! Noctu videbimus!"

Titus laughs, "Ah, those are just stories! We will see tonight!"

Villa prope silvam magnam et obscuram sita est. Incolae villae saepe dicunt silvam esse locum plenum spirituum, sed Gaius et familia sua haec non credunt.

The villa is located near a large and dark forest. The villa's inhabitants often say that the forest is a place full of spirits, but Gaius and his family do not believe this.

Sed nocte illa, sonitus miri in silva audiuntur.

But that night, strange sounds are heard in the forest.

Gaius, audax, clamat, "Amici, venite! Causam sonituum in silva explorabimus!"

Gaius, brave, shouts, "Friends, come! We will explore the cause of these sounds in the forest!"

Cum torchis et animis fortibus, Gaius et viri villae in silvam intrant. Titus et Lucius, curiosi, eos secreto sequuntur.

With torches and brave spirits, Gaius and the men of the villa enter the forest. Titus and Lucius, curious, secretly follow them.

Dum in silva ambulant, Lucius tremens dicit, "Tite, frigidum est et ventum... nox autem serena est!"

While walking in the forest, Lucius, trembling, says, "Titus, it's cold and windy... but the night is clear!"

Titus respondet, "Ssst! Audi! Quid est illud?"

Titus responds, "Shh! Listen! What is that?"

Repente, nebula densa eos circumdat. Omnes consistunt, et Gaius, serenus sed cautus, dicit, "Manete iuncti, ne nebula nos dividat!"

Suddenly, a thick fog surrounds them. Everyone stops, and Gaius, calm but cautious, says, "Stay together, so the fog doesn't separate us!"

Haec sunt prima mysteria quae nocte in silva emergunt. Quid in densa nebulosa futurum est? Sequens capitulum magis revelabit.

These are the first mysteries that emerge in the night within the forest. What will happen in the dense fog? The next chapter will reveal more.

Primae Apparitiones

Nebula in silva densior fit et visio omnium difficilior. Gaius et amici eius lampades accendunt, lumine tenui viam temptantes illustrare.

The fog in the forest grows thicker, and everyone's vision becomes more difficult. Gaius and his companions light their torches, trying to illuminate the path with dim light.

Dum procedunt, Lucius et Titus a maioribus paulum separantur. Lucius susurrat, "Tite, tardius incede! Nebula crassescit!"

As they proceed, Lucius and Titus get slightly separated from the adults. Lucius whispers, "Titus, slow down! The fog is thickening!"

Titus, curiosus, respondet, "Luci, vide! Quid illud est?"

Titus, curious, responds, "Lucius, look! What is that?"

Subito, ante Titum imago pallida apparet. Est figura feminae, quae flentis vultum habet. Lucius pallescens, "O dii," susurrat, "Femina est!"

Suddenly, a pale image appears before Titus. It is the figure of a woman with a weeping face. Lucius, turning pale, whispers, "Oh gods, it's a woman!"

Femina paulisper Titum et Lucium spectat, deinde in silvam silentio discedit. Titus, quamquam timet, animo movetur et dicit, "Sequere me, Luci. Sciendum est quid quaerat."

The woman gazes at Titus and Lucius for a moment, then silently moves deeper into the forest. Although afraid, Titus is moved and says, "Follow me, Lucius. We need to find out what she wants."

Lucius, dubitans, Titum sequitur. "Ubinam nos ducit?" quaerit.

Lucius, hesitant, follows Titus. "Where is she leading us?" he asks.

Femina per obscuras vias silvae eos ducit usque ad ruinam veterem. Ruinae sunt reliquiae domus antiquae, muris fractis et portis semirutis.

The woman leads them through the dark paths of the forest to an old ruin. The ruins are the remnants of an ancient house, with broken walls and half-ruined gates.

Interea, Gaius et reliqui viri in silva sonum clamoris audiunt. Gaius statim clamat, "Hoc auditis? Ad illud currere debemus!"

Meanwhile, Gaius and the other men hear a cry in the forest. Gaius immediately shouts, "Did you hear that? We must run to it!"

Omnes ad locum clamoris properant et ibi Titum et Lucium tremebundos inveniunt. Gaius, sollicitus, interrogat, "Quid accidit, fili?"

They all rush to the source of the cry and find Titus and Lucius trembling there. Gaius, concerned, asks, "What happened, son?"

Titus, respirans alte, narrat, "Pater, imago feminae... Nos ad hanc ruinam duxit. Flevit, ut videtur."

Titus, breathing deeply, explains, "Father, the image of a woman... She led us to these ruins. She seemed to be crying."

Gaius et viri circumspiciunt, sed nihil nisi ventum et umbras vident. Gaius dicit, "Domum revertamur. Hic nihil amplius agere possumus. Mane consilium capiemus."

Gaius and the men look around, but they see nothing but wind and shadows. Gaius says, "Let's return home. We can do nothing more here. We will make a plan in the morning."

Omnibus corde anxiis et mente plena quaestionibus, ad villam lentus regressus fit. In tenebris, cogitationes de visione nocturna et secretis silvae manent.

With hearts anxious and minds full of questions, they slowly return to the villa. In the darkness, thoughts of the nocturnal vision and the forest's secrets linger.

Res Investigantur

Die sequenti, post terrores noctis, Gaius in foro ambulat quaerens de historia loci. Senex, qui multa de vico scit, accedit et fabulam tragicam narrat.

The following day, after the terrors of the night, Gaius walks in the forum seeking information about the history of the place. An old man, who knows much about the village, approaches and tells a tragic tale.

Senex voce tremula incipit, "Antiqua domus in silva, olim locus laetitiae, sed nunc desolationis est. Familia ibi habitabat, cuius mater infortunio mortua est."

The old man begins with a trembling voice, "The old house in the forest, once a place of joy, is now one of desolation. A family lived there, but the mother died in misfortune."

Gaius, fronte contracta, respondet, "Saepe fabulae ex timore nascuntur. Nonne potest esse coincidentia?"

Gaius, with a furrowed brow, responds, "Stories often arise from fear. Could it not be just a coincidence?"

Senex caput movet, "Non, Gaie! Dicunt matrem adhuc in silva errare, filium suum quaerens."

The old man shakes his head, "No, Gaius! They say the mother still wanders in the forest, searching for her son."

Domum reversus, Gaius haec Marciae narrat. Sed Titus et Lucius, qui audierunt, inter se loquuntur.

Returning home, Gaius tells these things to Marcia. But Titus and Lucius, who overheard, speak among themselves.

Titus, serius quam solet, susurrat, "Luci, mater illa... spiritus esse potest."

Titus, more serious than usual, whispers, "Lucius, that mother... she could be a spirit."

Lucius, oculis magnis, "Vere credis? Nox proxima nobis res magis monstrabit."

Lucius, wide-eyed, responds, "Do you really believe that? The next night will show us more."

Ea nocte, sonitus externi rursus audiuntur. Gaius statim statuit, "Nunc oportet nos plura investigare. In silvam iterum ibimus."

That night, strange sounds are heard again. Gaius immediately decides, "Now we must investigate further. We will return to the forest."

Marcia, sollicita, "Gaie, cave! Silvae pericula magna habent."

Marcia, worried, says, "Gaius, be careful! The forest holds great dangers."

Gaius respondet, "Necesse est, Marcia. Mysteria solvere debemus."

Gaius replies, "It is necessary, Marcia. We must solve the mysteries."

Cum Gaius, armatus lampade et fide, in silvam ducit, Titus et Lucius, prohibiti venire, tamen sequuntur. Omnes magna cum cautela procedunt et ad ruinam domus iterum veniunt.

As Gaius, armed with a lamp and faith, leads into the forest, Titus and Lucius, though forbidden to come, follow anyway. All proceed with great caution and reach the ruins of the house once again.

In ruinis, inter lapides et herbas, vetus librum inveniunt. Titus, librum aperiens, "Ecce, liber! Fortasse responsa habet."

In the ruins, among the stones and grass, they find an old book. Titus, opening the book, says, "Look, a book! Perhaps it holds answers."

Liber, diarium matris mortuae, narrat de eius doloribus et spe filium suum rursus videndi. Scriptura tremula mater scripsit, "Unum desiderium habeo, filium meum iterum amplecti."

The book, a diary of the dead mother, tells of her sorrows and her hope of seeing her son again. In trembling writing, the mother wrote, "I have but one desire, to embrace my son again."

Gaius, libro lecto, "Haec femina, quam vidimus, mater dolorosa esse debet. Pro filio suo dolet."

Gaius, after reading the book, says, "This woman we saw must be the grieving mother. She mourns for her son."

Marcia, quae domi manet et pro eis orat, sola sedet, sperans eos tuto revenire. Noctis silentium et libri verba novam spem et metum familiae implent.

Marcia, who remains at home and prays for them, sits alone, hoping they return safely. The silence of the night and the words of the book fill the family with both new hope and fear.

Veritas Elucescit

Nocte tranquilla, sub luna clara, Gaius et familia librum matris legunt. Liber multas fabulas dolorum matris continet. Gaius, libro lecto, incipit credere spiritum verum esse.

On a calm night, under the bright moon, Gaius and his family read the mother's book. The book contains many tales of the mother's sorrows. After reading, Gaius begins to believe the spirit is real.

"Haec verba," Gaius dicit, "non fabulae videntur, sed verae doloris exclamationes."

"These words," Gaius says, "do not seem to be stories, but true cries of pain."

Dum de hoc disputant, repente, femina pallida rursus apparet ante domum. Hac vice, non solum Gaius et pueri, sed etiam Marcia eam vident.

While they discuss this, suddenly, the pale woman appears again in front of the house. This time, not only Gaius and the boys, but also Marcia see her.

Femina, voce tristi, "Filiolum meum quaero," loquitur.

The woman, in a sorrowful voice, says, "I seek my little son."

Titus, corde motus, "Quid tibi facere possumus?" rogat.

Titus, moved in his heart, asks, "What can we do for you?"

Gaius, feminae spectans, "Quomodo te adiuvare possumus?" dicit.

Gaius, looking at the woman, says, "How can we help you?"

Femina, "In libro," respondet, "est locus ubi filius meus requiescit."

The woman replies, "In the book, there is a place where my son rests."

Omnes ad librum festinant et paginam cum descriptione loci sepulturae filii legunt. Est locus sub arbore magna in silva.

They all hurry to the book and read the page with the description of the son's burial place. It is a spot under a large tree in the forest.

"Crastino," Gaius statuit, "ibimus et quaeremus."

"Tomorrow," Gaius decides, "we will go and search."

Luce prima, Gaius, Titus, Lucius, et aliqui amici viri ad locum designatum in silva pergunt. Sub arbore magna, terram effodiunt. Mox, parvum ossuarium inveniunt, ossa parvi pueri continentem.

At dawn, Gaius, Titus, Lucius, and a few trusted men go to the designated place in the forest. Under the great tree, they dig the ground. Soon, they find a small ossuary containing the bones of a young boy.

Cum ossuario, ad ruinam revertuntur. Femina, ossuarium videns, "Gratias vobis ago," dicit, lacrimans.

With the ossuary, they return to the ruins. The woman, seeing the ossuary, says, "Thank you," weeping.

Deinde, lumine circumfusa, spiritus matris in aere clarescit et paulatim evanescit.

Then, surrounded by light, the mother's spirit shines in the air and slowly fades away.

Titus, spectans, "Pacem sentio, quasi finis doloris venit," dicit.

Titus, watching, says, "I feel peace, as if the pain has come to an end."

Gaius, ad familiam vertens, "Hodie bonum opus fecimus," affirmat.

Gaius, turning to his family, says, "Today we have done a good deed."

Nocte illa, omnes in villa tranquilli dormiunt, sensum pacis profundae sentientes, scientes spiritum matris nunc requiem habere.

That night, everyone sleeps peacefully in the villa, feeling a deep sense of peace, knowing the mother's spirit now has found rest.

Consequuntur

Mane post noctem pacis, in villa, familia laetior surgit. Gaius, Marcia, Titus, et Lucius in triclinio simul prandent. Marcia, serenior quam antea, inquit, "Nox mira fuit, sed cor meum levius est."

The morning after the peaceful night, the family rises happier. Gaius, Marcia, Titus, and Lucius dine together in the dining room. Marcia, calmer than before, says, "It was a strange night, but my heart feels lighter."

Sed Gaius, libro adhuc in mente, subito dicit, "Est aliquid amplius in libro. Non solum mater, sed etiam spiritus alter invenitur."

But Gaius, still thinking about the book, suddenly says, "There is something more in the book. It is not just the mother; another spirit is mentioned."

Titus, attentus, rogat, "Quis est?"

Titus, listening carefully, asks, "Who is it?"

Gaius explicat, "Spiritus patris familiae, qui periit. In silva a latronibus occisus est."

Gaius explains, "The spirit of the father of the family, who died. He was killed by robbers in the forest."

Titus et Lucius sese aspiciunt, trepidatione affecti. Lucius quaerit, "Nonne ille requiem habet?"

Titus and Lucius look at each other, filled with fear. Lucius asks, "Does he not have peace?"

Gaius caput movet, "Non, spiritus eius iratus est. Mortem violentam habuit et pacem non invenit."

Gaius shakes his head, "No, his spirit is angry. He died a violent death and has not found peace."

Titus, animo consternato, inquit, "Quid facere oportet, pater?"

Titus, shocked, says, "What should we do, father?"

Gaius respondet, "Nocte iterum in silvam ibimus, spiritum patris quaerentes."

Gaius replies, "Tonight we will go into the forest again, seeking the father's spirit."

Cum nox venit, Gaius, Titus, et Lucius, armati lampadibus, ad silvam iterum vadunt. In umbra arborum, spiritus patris repente apparens, iratus et tristis, exclamat, "Iustitiam volo!"

When night falls, Gaius, Titus, and Lucius, armed with torches, go into the forest again. In the shadow of the trees, the father's spirit suddenly appears, angry and sad, shouting, "I want justice!"

Gaius, spiritum spectans, dicit, "Promitto, te adiuvabo. Qui te occiderunt, punientur."

Gaius, looking at the spirit, says, "I promise, I will help you. Those who killed you will be punished."

Reversi domum, Gaius vetustos annales villae explorat. Cum Lucio et Tito, scripta vetera pervolvunt et nomina latronum et eorum descendentium inveniunt.

After returning home, Gaius explores the old records of the villa. Together with Lucius and Titus, they search through the old writings and find the names of the robbers and their descendants.

Die sequenti, Gaius cum magistratu convenit. Gaius magistratui explicat, "Haec sunt nomina latronum et hi sunt descendentes. Iustitiam quaerimus."

The next day, Gaius meets with the magistrate. Gaius explains to the magistrate, "These are the names of the robbers and these are their descendants. We seek justice."

Magistratus, rebus consideratis, promissionem dat, "Actio iuridica fiet. Iustitia servabitur."

The magistrate, after considering the matter, gives his promise, "Legal action will be taken. Justice will be served."

Gaius, gratus, domum redit et familiae nuntiat, "Iustitia mox fiet. Spiritus tandem pacem inveniet." Omnes in familia spe et expectatione pleni sunt, finem doloris patris et totius familiae exspectantes.

Gaius, grateful, returns home and announces to his family, "Justice will soon be done. The spirit will finally find peace." The whole family is full of hope and anticipation, awaiting the end of the father's pain and the peace of the entire family.

Resolutio

Sol clarus lucet cum Gaius et familia cum magistratu et custodibus conveniunt. In atrio magno villae, descendentes latronum, qui in villa vivunt, adsunt, ignari de criminibus maiorum.

The bright sun shines as Gaius and his family meet with the magistrate and guards. In the large courtyard of the villa, the descendants of the robbers, who live in the villa, are present, unaware of the crimes of their ancestors.

Gaius, tranquillus sed firmus, inquit, "De iniuriis veteribus hodie loquimur." Descendentes, solliciti, audiunt.

Gaius, calm but firm, says, "Today we speak of old wrongs." The descendants, anxious, listen.

Magistratus, serius, explicat, "Iniustitiae patrum vestrorum hic explicabuntur. Oportet nos de reconciliatione agere."

The magistrate, serious, explains, "The injustices of your fathers will be explained here. We must seek reconciliation."

Unus ex descendentibus, voce tremula, respondet, "Ignorabamus de his criminibus. Poenitet nos doloris quem patres nostri causaverunt."

One of the descendants, with a trembling voice, responds, "We did not know about these crimes. We are sorry for the pain our fathers caused."

Gaius, considerate, dicit, "Poenitentia vestra accepta est. Nunc de pace agere debemus."

Gaius, thoughtfully, says, "Your repentance is accepted. Now we must act for peace."

Nocte illa, familia et omnes ad silvam iterum vadunt. Spiritus patris, nunc pacatus et gratus, apparet.

That night, the family and everyone go to the forest again. The spirit of the father, now peaceful and grateful, appears.

"Satis est," spiritus dicit. "Pax mea nunc plena est. Gratias vobis omnibus."

"It is enough," the spirit says. "My peace is now complete. Thank you all."

Gaius, cum familia, sacrificium pro pacatione spirituum facit. Prope arborem magnam, ubi ossuarium reconditum erat, sacrificium ponunt.

Gaius, with his family, performs a sacrifice for the calming of the spirits. Near the great tree, where the ossuary was placed, they offer the sacrifice.

Cum sacrificium finiunt, lumen clarum supra silvam videtur. Spiritus matris et patris simul apparent. "Nunc quiescimus. Pax nostra vobiscum," dicunt.

When they finish the sacrifice, a bright light is seen above the forest. The spirits of the mother and father appear together. "Now we rest. Our peace is with you," they say.

Cum verba finiunt, ambo in luce clara ascendunt et nebula, quae per tot annos silvam obscuraverat, dissolvitur.

When the words are finished, both ascend into the bright light, and the mist that had covered the forest for so many years dissolves.

Titus, ad Gaium spectans, dicit, "Pater, silva nunc libera est, ut nos."

Titus, looking at Gaius, says, "Father, the forest is now free, like us."

Gaius, omnes amplectens, inquit, "Pacem longam habemus. Gratias agamus pro hac nocte, pro hoc fine."

Gaius, embracing everyone, says, "We have long peace. Let us give thanks for this night, for this ending."

Villa et silva, post haec eventa, pacem longam et serenam habent. Omnes incolae sentiunt mutationem et in futurum tranquilli vivunt.

The villa and forest, after these events, enjoy a long and serene peace. All the inhabitants feel the change and live peacefully into the future.

Spectra Alexandrina

Adventus et Apparitio

Caesar cum suis militibus ad portus Alexandriae appropinquavit. Mare tranquillum, caelum serenum erat. Dum navis ad terram appropinquabat, Caesar Cleopatrae de adventu suo per nuntium scripserat. Urbs plena tumultu bellique signis erat.

Caesar, with his soldiers, approached the ports of Alexandria. The sea was calm, and the sky was clear. As the ship neared the shore, Caesar had sent a message to Cleopatra about his arrival. The city was full of turmoil and signs of war.

Nox venit, Caesar, regiam intramus?" quaesivit legatus.

"Night is coming, Caesar. Do we enter the palace?" asked the envoy.

"Ita," respondit Caesar, "intra muros tuti erimus." Dum per obscuros urbis vicos incedebant, subito, in horto palatii, spiritus apparet.

"Yes," Caesar responded, "we will be safe inside the walls." As they walked through the dark streets of the city, suddenly, a spirit appeared in the palace garden.

"Spectaculumne hoc est?" milites murmurerunt, pallidi et trementes.

"Is this some kind of show?" the soldiers murmured, pale and trembling.

Spiritus, forma mulieris Aegyptiae, ante eos stetit et voce flebili locuta est, "Grave futurum porto."

The spirit, in the form of an Egyptian woman, stood before them and spoke in a sorrowful voice, "I bring a grave future."

Caesar, spiritum intuens, manu gestum pacis fecit. "Quis es? Quid vis?" rogavit.

Caesar, gazing at the spirit, made a gesture of peace with his hand. "Who are you? What do you want?" he asked.

"Ego sum quae praeterita regni memoria teneo," respondit spiritus. "Maledictum in regno vestro manet."

"I am the one who holds the memory of the kingdom's past," the spirit responded. "A curse remains upon your kingdom."

"Maledictum?" Cleopatra, subito adveniens, interpellavit. "De quo loqueris?"

"A curse?" Cleopatra, suddenly arriving, interrupted. "What are you talking about?"

Spiritus ad Cleopatram conversus est. "Regina, scisne de antiquo maledicto quod patriam tuam gravat?"

The spirit turned to Cleopatra. "Queen, do you know of the ancient curse that burdens your land?"

Cleopatra, sollicita, caput inclinavit. "Ita, fabulas audivi... sed num verae sunt?"

Cleopatra, worried, nodded her head. "Yes, I have heard the stories... but are they true?"

"Verissimae, regina. Et nisi solvitur, ruinam omnibus afferet," explicavit spiritus.

"Most true, my queen. And unless it is broken, it will bring ruin to all," explained the spirit.

"Misere nobis!" exclamavit Cleopatra. "Quid facere debemus?"

"Woe to us!" Cleopatra exclaimed. "What must we do?"

"Libros sacros consule, Cleopatra. Sacerdotes etiam auguresque convoca. Solum ritu antiquo maledictum solvi potest," consilium dedit spiritus.

"Consult the sacred books, Cleopatra. Also summon the priests and augurs. Only through an ancient ritual can the curse be broken," advised the spirit.

Caesar, spiritu et Cleopatra auditis, statuit, "Faciamus. Noctem non exspectemus. Agite!"

Caesar, having heard the spirit and Cleopatra, decided, "Let's do it. We won't wait for night. Let's go!"

Concursu ad palatium, Caesar et Cleopatra parati erant ad maledictum investigandum et, si possent, ad pacem perpetuam restituendam.

Rushing to the palace, Caesar and Cleopatra were ready to investigate the curse and, if possible, to restore everlasting peace.

Obsidio et Omina

Caesar, copiis suis imperans, ad urbem Alexandriam properat. Pompeianos oppugnaturus, urbem cingit. Muri alti, portae graves. Obsidio incipit.

Caesar, commanding his troops, hastens to the city of Alexandria. About to attack the Pompeians, he surrounds the city. The walls are high, the gates heavy. The siege begins.

"Nocte hac spiritus iterum visus est!" exclamat miles, pavore plenus.

"This night the spirit was seen again!" a soldier exclaims, full of fear.

"Spiritus hic nobis quid dicit?" Caesar interrogat, dum per vallum ambulat.

"What does this spirit tell us?" Caesar asks as he walks through the rampart.

"In somniis loquitur," respondet miles. "Dolorum finem promittit."

"It speaks in dreams," the soldier replies. "It promises an end to sorrows."

Eodem tempore, in urbe fames et sitis crescit. Populus laborat, spes minuitur.

At the same time, hunger and thirst increase in the city. The people struggle, hope diminishes.

"Videmusne iterum spiritum?" Cleopatra, sollicita, Caesarem rogat.

"Do we see the spirit again?" Cleopatra, worried, asks Caesar.

"Saepe in undis," respondet Caesar. "Navali proelio apparuit. Nostri milites, viso eo, fortius pugnant."

"Often in the waves," Caesar replies. "It appeared in the naval battle. Our soldiers, seeing it, fight more bravely."

Pompeiani, audientes et videntes spiritum, territi sunt. Nonnulli eorum proelia deserunt.

The Pompeians, hearing and seeing the spirit, are terrified. Some of them abandon the battles.

"Nocte, spiritus ad me venit," Caesar secreto Cleopatrae narrat. "Viam ad victoriam mihi ostendit."

"At night, the spirit came to me," Caesar secretly tells Cleopatra. "It showed me the path to victory."

"Mirabile!" Cleopatra exclamat. "Quid faciemus?"

"Amazing!" Cleopatra exclaims. "What shall we do?"

"Crastino die, sacrificium Aegyptium parabimus," Caesar statuit. "Spiritus pacem et auxilium promisit."

"Tomorrow, we will prepare an Egyptian sacrifice," Caesar decides. "The spirit promised peace and help."

Ad regna vicina nuntii missi sunt, auxilium quaerentes. In itinere, spiritus eis apparet, signum bonum portans.

Messengers were sent to neighboring kingdoms, seeking help. On the way, the spirit appeared to them, bringing a good omen.

Dies difficiles urbem premebant, sed Caesar et Cleopatra, renovata spe, consilia capiunt. Sacrificium magna cum cura paratur.

Difficult days pressed upon the city, but Caesar and Cleopatra, with renewed hope, make plans. The sacrifice is prepared with great care.

"Nox venit, sacrificium incipiemus," Cleopatra dicit. Caesar, milites, et sacerdotes ad templum conveniunt.

"Night has come, we will begin the sacrifice," Cleopatra says. Caesar, the soldiers, and the priests gather at the temple.

Spiritus, sacrificio appropinquante, clarus et serenus apparet. "Pacem vobis fero, si ritus recte perficitur," spiritus loquitur.

As the sacrifice approaches, the spirit appears, bright and serene. "I bring you peace, if the ritual is performed correctly," the spirit speaks.

Caesar et omnes qui aderant, ritum sollemniter exsequuntur, pacem deorum et spirituum sperantes. Spe renovata, omnes in futurum melius nituntur.

Caesar and all those present solemnly perform the ritual, hoping for the peace of the gods and spirits. With renewed hope, everyone strives for a better future.

Victoria et Veritas

In castris Romanis, Caesar vigilat. Subito, nuntius accurrit.

In the Roman camp, Caesar watches. Suddenly, a messenger runs in.

"Domine, Pompeiani consilia nova struunt!" nuntius exclamat.

"Lord, the Pompeians are devising new plans!" the messenger exclaims.

"Quid consiliant?" Caesar sereno animo interrogat.

"What are they planning?" Caesar asks with a calm mind.

"Vires tuas debilitare cupiunt, per insidias," nuntius respondet.

"They wish to weaken your forces through ambushes," the messenger responds.

"Spiritusne quid dixit?" Caesar rogat, quia spiritu saepe fretus est.

"Has the spirit said anything?" Caesar asks, as he often relies on the spirit.

"Sic, domine. Insidias praevidit. Caute agendum est," nuntius confirmat.

"Yes, lord. It foresaw the ambush. We must act cautiously," the messenger confirms.

"Nocte hac, spiritus iterum apparuit," Caesar militem alloquitur.

"This night, the spirit appeared again," Caesar speaks to the soldier.

"Quid nobis monuit?" Caesar curiosus est.

"What did it warn us about?" Caesar is curious.

"Agmina ad loca clavis Pompeianorum dirigere debemus. Ibi sunt debiles," miles explicat.

"We must direct our troops to the key positions of the Pompeians. There they are weak," the soldier explains.

"Age! Proelia parate!" Caesar milites incitat. Cum magno clamore, Romani proelia in urbem gerunt. Sensim progrediuntur.

"Go! Prepare for battle!" Caesar urges the soldiers. With a great shout, the Romans wage war in the city. They advance steadily.

Interea, in regia, Cleopatra anxie exspectat. Spiritus repente apparet.

Meanwhile, in the palace, Cleopatra waits anxiously. The spirit suddenly appears.

"O regina," spiritus incipit, "secretum tibi revelabo."

"O queen," the spirit begins, "I will reveal a secret to you."

Cleopatra attentat. "Dic mihi, quaeso."

Cleopatra listens attentively. "Tell me, please."

"De tua familia est... de antiqua maledictione," spiritus somberly enuntiat.

"It is about your family... about an ancient curse," the spirit solemnly declares.

"Maledictum? Quod urbi imminet?" Cleopatra sollicita interrogat.

"A curse? One that threatens the city?" Cleopatra asks anxiously.

"Ita. In templum antiquum te ducam, ubi solutio est," spiritus promittit.

"Yes. I will lead you to the ancient temple, where the solution lies," the spirit promises.

Caesar, reversus ex proelio, et Cleopatra ad templum ducuntur. Ibi, ritus solvendi maledictum incipiunt. Sacerdotes sacrificia offerunt, preces murmurant.

Caesar, having returned from battle, and Cleopatra are led to the temple. There, the rituals to break the curse begin. The priests offer sacrifices, murmuring prayers.

Dum ritus perficitur, spiritus historiam suam narrat. "Regina eram, iniuste de throno deiecta, maledicta. Nunc, maledictum solvere potes."

As the ritual is performed, the spirit tells its story. "I was a queen, unjustly dethroned, cursed. Now, you can break the curse."

Cum ritus finitur, tranquillitas mirabilis templum implet. "Pacem inveni," spiritus serena voce dicit, et evanescit.

When the ritual ends, a miraculous peace fills the temple. "I have found peace," the spirit says in a serene voice, and vanishes.

Urbs et exercitus tranquillitatem recipiunt, spiritu soluto. Pompeiani, sine spiritu, confusi sunt.

The city and the army regain peace, as the spirit is released. The Pompeians, without the spirit, are confused.

"Victoria nostra est," Caesar ad milites clamat. "Alexandriam plene cepimus!" Romani laetantur, urbe capta. Pax tandem redit, veritas revelata, spiritus liberatus.

"Victory is ours," Caesar shouts to the soldiers. "We have fully captured Alexandria!" The Romans rejoice, with the city captured. Peace finally returns, truth revealed, and the spirit set free.

Res Novae

Caesar et Cleopatra, post victoriam celebratam, Alexandriam ingressi sunt.

Caesar and Cleopatra, after celebrating the victory, entered Alexandria.

Urbis aspectum mutare statuerunt.

They decided to change the appearance of the city.

"Videmus ruinas passim," Cleopatra Caesari dicit, per urbis vias ambulantes. "Reaedificare debemus."

"We see ruins everywhere," Cleopatra says to Caesar as they walk through the streets of the city. "We must rebuild."

"Et aedificabimus," Caesar respondet. "Nova structura, nova spes."

"And we will build," Caesar replies. "New structures, new hope."

Opera magna inchoantur. Muri diruti reficiuntur, domus novae exstruuntur.

Great works begin. The destroyed walls are repaired, new houses are built.

"Populus de spiritu saepe loquitur," Cleopatra narrat. "Eius historia nos docet."

"The people often speak of the spirit," Cleopatra says. "Its story teaches us."

"Docet et unum facit," Caesar addit. "Pax inter nos firmior fiet."

"It teaches and unites," Caesar adds. "The peace between us will become stronger."

Cleopatra caput assentitur. "Leges novas promulgare debemus, ut iustitia et pax maneant."

Cleopatra nods. "We must enact new laws, so that justice and peace may remain."

"Ita," Caesar concordat. "Aequitas omnes regat."

"Yes," Caesar agrees. "Equity must rule everyone."

Negotiatores Romani et Aegyptii frequentius conveniunt. Mercatus crescit, commercia florent.

Roman and Egyptian merchants meet more frequently. The market grows, trade flourishes.

"Docti et artifices veniunt," Cleopatra laeta est. "Scholas magnas aedificabimus."

"Scholars and artisans are coming," Cleopatra says happily. "We will build great schools."

"Et academias," Caesar subridens dicit. "Ubi iuvenes discant et crescant."

"And academies," Caesar says with a smile. "Where young people can learn and grow."

In memoria spiritus, festum magni momenti instituunt. "Eius pacem celebramus," Cleopatra populo annuntiat.

In memory of the spirit, they establish a great festival. "We celebrate its peace," Cleopatra announces to the people.

Caesar et Cleopatra templum novo deo, deo pacis, dedicant. "Hic deus nos protegat," Caesar orans dicit.

Caesar and Cleopatra dedicate a temple to a new god, the god of peace. "May this god protect us," Caesar says in prayer.

Nuntii per imperium diffunduntur. "Pax et prosperitas," nuntii clamant.

Messengers spread the news throughout the empire. "Peace and prosperity," they proclaim.

Post haec, Caesar milites suos parat. "Tempus est redire," dicit. "Opera pacis manent."

After this, Caesar prepares his soldiers. "It is time to return," he says. "The work of peace remains."

"In templo spiritus manebit," Cleopatra addit. "Locum sacrum habebimus, ubi eum memoremus."

"In the temple, the spirit will remain," Cleopatra adds. "We will have a sacred place where we remember him."

Alexandria, lumine novo fulgens, pharus mundi rursus fit.

Alexandria, shining with new light, becomes once again a beacon to the world.

"Lux culturae et scientiae," Cleopatra aspicit et subridet. "Nova aetas incepit."

"A light of culture and science," Cleopatra observes and smiles. "A new age has begun."

Umbra Hannibalis

In Italiae Oris

Nocte Romae, sub luna plena, spectrum Hannibalis apparet. In castris Romanorum, somnia militum terrent. "Quis ibi est?" miles tremens interrogat, sed responsa nulla sunt. Signa militaria sine vento moventur; tumultus et clamores sine causa audiri possunt.

At night in Rome, under the full moon, the specter of Hannibal appears. In the Roman camps, the soldiers' dreams are disturbed. "Who is there?" a trembling soldier asks, but there is no answer. The military standards move without wind; commotions and cries can be heard without cause.

Subito, equi Romanorum territi sunt. "Ecce, Hannibal ad Pontem Milvium!" exclamat vigilia. Hannibal Romanos provocat, stans super pontem, figura obscura et terribilis.

Suddenly, the Roman horses are frightened. "Look, Hannibal at the Milvian Bridge!" the watchman shouts. Hannibal challenges the Romans, standing on the bridge, a dark and terrifying figure.

Praetor Romanus, Marcellus nomine, apparitionem investigare statuit. "Custodes ad pontem mittite," praetor iubet. Custodes armati ad Pontem Milvium nocte media vadunt.

The Roman praetor, named Marcellus, decides to investigate the apparition. "Send the guards to the bridge," orders the praetor. Armed guards go to the Milvian Bridge in the middle of the night.

"Videsne hoc?" custos dicit, gladium in terra sine manu tenentem ostendens. Dum spectant, risu horrendo Hannibalis circumdantur.

"Do you see this?" says a guard, pointing to a sword held in the ground without a hand. While they watch, they are surrounded by Hannibal's horrifying laughter.

"Cur hic es?" praetor in somnio Hannibalem interrogat, ubi Hannibal bellum gerit.

"Why are you here?" the praetor asks Hannibal in a dream, where Hannibal wages war.

"Sequere me," Hannibal spectrum in somnio praetori imperat, voce gravi.

"Follow me," the specter of Hannibal commands the praetor in the dream, in a deep voice.

Marcellus expergiscitur, perterritus. "Libros Sibyllinos consulemus!" Marcellus suadet. Sed cum libri consuluntur, responsa obscura sunt: "Umbra ductoris sequenda est."

Marcellus wakes up, terrified. "We will consult the Sibylline books!" Marcellus suggests. But when the books are consulted, the responses are unclear: "The shadow of the leader must be followed."

"Sequimur umbrae imperium," Marcellus solus statuit. Hannibal spectrum iterum apparens, "Venite," susurrat, vento portatus.

"We follow the shadow's command," Marcellus decides alone. Hannibal's specter appears again, whispering, "Come," carried by the wind.

Hannibalis umbra Romanos in novam et miram historiam ducit, plenam mysteriis et timore, sed etiam fortitudine et casu. Romanis res nova est, sed Hannibalis spectrum iam pridem scit quae ventura sunt.

The shadow of Hannibal leads the Romans into a new and strange story, full of mysteries and fear, but also of bravery and fate. For the Romans, it is something new, but Hannibal's specter has long known what is to come.

Umbrae Bellum

Praetor Marcellus cum legionibus spectrum Hannibalis sequitur. Dum iter faciunt, viae ante eos mutantur, spectri ductu.

Praetor Marcellus follows the specter of Hannibal with his legions. As they journey, the roads before them change, guided by the specter.

In silvis, arbores moveri videntur, velut in pugna antiqua. "Videsne illas arbores?" miles susurrat. Alter respondet, "Magia est, sine dubio!"

In the forests, the trees seem to move, as if in an ancient battle. "Do you see those trees?" a soldier whispers. Another replies, "It is magic, without a doubt!"

Noctu, Marcellus somnia terribilia habet. In somnis, Hannibal minans apparet. "Relinque terras meas," Hannibal clamat.

At night, Marcellus has terrible dreams. In his sleep, Hannibal appears threatening. "Leave my lands," Hannibal shouts.

Prope castra, flumina rubescunt. "Sanguis est?" miles exclamat, aquam spectans. Alter miles, "Spectra!" susurrat.

Near the camp, the rivers turn red. "Is it blood?" a soldier exclaims, staring at the water. Another soldier whispers, "Specters!"

Ventus voces Punicas afferre videtur. "Audisne illas voces?" quaerit Marcellus. "Punicas voces! Num Hannibal nobiscum loquitur?"

The wind seems to carry Punic voices. "Do you hear those voices?" Marcellus asks. "Punic voices! Is Hannibal speaking to us?"

Dum castra Romanorum nebulosa sunt, spectra militum Punicorum videntur. "Hic manes sunt," praetor dicit, "timere non debemus!"

While the Roman camp is covered in mist, the specters of Punic soldiers appear. "These are spirits," the praetor says, "we must not fear!"

Tactus frigus omnes sentiunt, etiam sub sole ardente. "Frigus hoc... non naturale est," Marcellus murmurat.

Everyone feels a touch of cold, even under the burning sun. "This cold... is not natural," Marcellus murmurs.

Subito, equus praetoris ad Carthaginis antiquae situm currit. "Quo vadis, o bone equus?" Marcellus equum tenens rogat.

Suddenly, the praetor's horse runs toward the ancient site of Carthage. "Where are you going, good horse?" Marcellus asks, holding the reins.

In campo, arma antiqua effodiuntur. "Haec arma! Ex tempore Hannibalis!" exclamat miles.

In the field, ancient weapons are unearthed. "These weapons! From the time of Hannibal!" a soldier exclaims.

Nocte, ignei globi castra Romanorum circumdant. "Quae sunt haec lumina?" miles trepidus quaerit.

At night, fiery globes surround the Roman camp. "What are these lights?" a frightened soldier asks.

Marcellus, desperatus, exorare Hannibalis manes temptat. "Hannibal, quid vis a nobis?" clamat in silvam.

Marcellus, desperate, tries to plead with Hannibal's spirit. "Hannibal, what do you want from us?" he shouts into the forest.

E silva, magna voce, manes respondet, "Venite et videbitis!" Marcellus, audens, "Sequemur," dicit.

From the forest, in a loud voice, the spirit responds, "Come and you will see!" Marcellus, daring, says, "We will follow."

Legionibus Romanis sequentibus, Hannibal spectrum eos ad locum plenum mysteriis et historiae ducit, ubi terra ipsa cum manibus antiquis loquitur.

With the Roman legions following, Hannibal's specter leads them to a place full of mysteries and history, where the land itself speaks with ancient hands.

Proelia Nocturna

Spectrum Hannibalis Romanos ad montem altum ducit. Nebula densa undique montem circumdat. "Venite!" Hannibal per nubem clamat. Marcellus et milites, metu capti, in nebula procedunt.

The specter of Hannibal leads the Romans to a high mountain. A thick mist surrounds the mountain on all sides. "Come!" Hannibal shouts through the cloud. Marcellus and the soldiers, gripped by fear, advance into the mist.

"Quid videmus?" miles tremens Marcellum interrogat, formis armatorum in nebula apparentibus. "Manes antiquorum militum sunt," Marcellus respondet.

"What are we seeing?" a trembling soldier asks Marcellus, as shapes of armed men appear in the mist. "They are the spirits of ancient soldiers," Marcellus replies.

Clamores et sonitus ferri deinde audiri possunt. "Pugnas veterum audimus!" alter miles exclamat. Subito, umbrae contra Romanos pugnare incipiunt. "Fugite!" miles clamat, sed viae clausae sunt.

Shouts and the clashing of iron can then be heard. "We hear the battles of old!" another soldier exclaims. Suddenly, the shadows begin to fight against the Romans. "Flee!" a soldier shouts, but the paths are blocked.

Spectrum Hannibalis Romanis non amplius apparet, sed eius vox manet. "Non effugietis," vox per nubes tonat. Praetor ab umbra sine corpore corripitur. "Quis me tenet?" Marcellus clamitat, nullo vidente.

The specter of Hannibal no longer appears to the Romans, but his voice remains. "You will not escape," the voice thunders through the clouds. The praetor is seized by a bodiless shadow. "Who is holding me?" Marcellus shouts, seeing no one.

Nox plena fulgoribus et tonitribus est, umbrae lucem diemque simulant, sed sol non apparet. "Nox aeterna nobis est!" milites clamant.

The night is full of flashes and thunder, the shadows mimicking light and day, but the sun does not appear. "It is an eternal night for us!" the soldiers cry out.

Militum nonnulli a spectris capti sunt, subito in aere suspensi. "Liberate nos!" capti clamant. Exercitus Romanus sine ducibus in confusionem inducitur.

Some soldiers are seized by the specters, suddenly suspended in the air. "Free us!" the captives shout. The Roman army, without its leaders, falls into confusion.

Cum prima lux apparet, umbrae repente evanescunt. Marcellus, magna levatione affectus, dicit, "Salvi sumus." Milites, exhausti sed vivi, in castra revertuntur, mirantes quae nocte acciderint.

When the first light appears, the shadows suddenly vanish. Marcellus, deeply relieved, says, "We are saved." The soldiers, exhausted but alive, return to the camp, wondering what had happened during the night.

Hannibalis Victoria

Exercitus Romanorum fractus est. Hannibalis spectrum praetori Marcello iterum apparet. "Quid vis a nobis?" Marcellus, desperatus, Hannibalem interrogat.

The Roman army is broken. The specter of Hannibal appears again to Praetor Marcellus. "What do you want from us?" Marcellus, desperate, asks Hannibal.

"Arma vestra deponite," Hannibal imperat. Marcellus, secum cogitans, legatos ad Hannibalem mittit, pacem petentes.

"Lay down your arms," Hannibal commands. Marcellus, reflecting to himself, sends envoys to Hannibal, seeking peace.

"Quid nobis ostendis?" legatus Hannibalem interrogat. Spectrum Romanis somnia ostendit, in quibus semper a spectris victi sunt.

"What do you show us?" the envoy asks Hannibal. The specter shows the Romans dreams in which they are always defeated by specters.

"Finem belli volumus," Hannibal postulat. Marcellus, agnoscens victoriam Hannibalis, arma in terra deponit et fidelitatem spectri iurat.

"We want the war to end," Hannibal demands. Marcellus, acknowledging Hannibal's victory, lays down his arms on the ground and swears allegiance to the specter.

"Sequimini me," Hannibal dicit, et Romanos ad antiquas Carthaginis ruinas ducit. Subito, quasi magia, ruinae resurgunt, urbs nova ante oculos apparet.

"Follow me," Hannibal says, and leads the Romans to the ancient ruins of Carthage. Suddenly, as if by magic, the ruins rise again, and a new city appears before their eyes.

"Videte! Carthago resurgit!" Hannibal exclamat. Spectra Carthaginiensium per vias novae urbis ambulant, vivi et mortui in unum locum coeunt.

"Look! Carthage rises again!" Hannibal exclaims. The specters of Carthaginians walk through the streets of the new city, the living and the dead gathering in one place.

Fines imperii Romani recedunt, et nova Carthago in potestate spectri Hannibalis apparet. Spectrum risu victor in lucem solis evanescit.

The borders of the Roman Empire recede, and the new Carthage appears under the control of Hannibal's specter. The specter, laughing victoriously, vanishes into the sunlight.

"Pax est inter nos et umbras," Marcellus, pacem acceptans, dicit. Pax inter vivos et mortuos nunc promittitur, imperium novum sub umbris et hominibus.

"There is peace between us and the shadows," Marcellus says, accepting peace. Peace is now promised between the living and the dead, a new empire under both shadows and men.

Milites Romanorum, nova realitate accepta, ad suas domos revertuntur, historia mirabili narranda.

The Roman soldiers, having accepted this new reality, return to their homes with an incredible story to tell.

More books

More ressources

Endorsements by leading Latinists

All on discoverlatin.com